the complete manual of

racing and betting

systems

the complete manual of

racing and betting

systems

david duncan

foulsham
LONDON • NEW YORK • TORONTO • SYDNEY

foulsham

The Publishing House, Bennetts Close, Cippenham, Berkshire, SL1 5AP, England

ISBN 0-572-02695-1

Printed in Great Britain by St Edmundsbury Press, Bury St Edmunds, Suffolk

Contents

Betting and You

Racing is more popular now than ever before. All kinds of people follow the Sport of Kings. Betting shops offer greater comfort and improved facilities and take their place in every high street. Betting is now a respectable pastime and every major meeting receives extensive television coverage. Small wonder that betting turnover has reached record levels, even allowing for inflation. While other spectator sports experience difficulties, racing has consolidated its position and challenges soccer as our national sport.

Also, racing has become international to an extent undreamt of a quarter of a century ago. An English champion racehorse can no longer claim pre-eminence unless it can prove itself in the Breeders' Cup series of races in America in the autumn of each year. British horses now routinely undertake an annual antipodean journey to challenge for Australia's greatest race, the Melbourne Cup, which is a handicap over two miles, whilst the goings-on in the Dubai desert at Nad Al Sheba in March offer instant world recognition and fabulous sums in prize money and make racing a truly global contest.

The pages that follow are mostly about racing at home, and you have no doubt purchased this book because you like a bet in that arena. If you are honest you will almost certainly admit that you lose in the long run. Most people do and the reason is simple. Unlike the bookmaker who bets along methodical, businesslike lines, the average punter stakes haphazardly according to fancy. This is fatal and plays right into the bookmaker's hands. If, on the other hand, you are prepared to study the form book or follow systems based on established patterns of form and statistics, you give yourself a chance of winning.

No judge of form and no system can pick a winner every time and even the best methods are unlikely to yield more than a marginal gain on outlay but that is still a lot better than losing. Methodical betting along form or systematic lines, although it cannot guarantee success, offers a real prospect of a winning balance.

This book has four parts. Each constitutes a vital element in the armoury of the betting enthusiast who is fully equipped for the battle with the bookmaker.

Part 1 is a complete guide to reading the form book based on the author's own unique method of calculating chances. There is a method of instant handicapping which offers an alternative to conventional techniques of trying to beat the handicapper. In addition, there is a series of shortcuts to winner-finding, arranged according to the type of race to be assessed. Criteria 1 to 24 can, for the most part, be operated by simple reference to a morning newspaper without the necessity of getting involved in a deeper study of form. However, the wise racing fan will probably do best by blending the various guidelines with an analysis of form to arrive at selections with the optimum chance of success.

Whatever strategy or techniques you adopt though, you will be in a position to contemplate a full day's betting at several meetings or the particular card for a meeting you are attending with confidence about your ability to pick out the best bets that were very likely totally alien to you hitherto.

In Part 2, 12 automatic racing systems are explained. Why 12 when one winning method will do? The answer is that different styles of betting appeal to different people. So you will find in these pages systems for the Flat and systems for the jumps. There are plans for favourites and plans for longer-priced selections. Most focus on win-only betting, but those who feel happier with each-way investments are also accommodated. A few go a stage further and are solely concerned with the staking as opposed to the selection aspect of backing horses. There is an attempt to exploit the excellent racing coverage to be found in the national press. In fact, the 12 systems featured in the following pages cover the whole spectrum of racing. Whatever your betting preferences, you will find something here to interest you.

Each plan has full operating instructions and can be understood by anyone who has only a rudimentary knowledge of racing and betting. On the other hand the book as a whole, though easy to follow, is written from the expert point of view. Some experts scoff at systems. They point out that horses are not machines, that every system can be beaten sooner or later by the long losing run, that the bookmaker always wins in the end, and so on. Now it is certainly true that racing is notoriously unpredictable with the odds stacked against the punter and for these reasons no one should ever bet more than they can afford to lose on a system, however good it may appear.

Having said that, it is my belief that for the average punter who has no inside knowledge of the operations of a racing stable and no clue about secrets which are always jealously guarded, logical betting, according to some plan based on racing know-how and horse sense, offers the best chance of winning at a pastime which inevitably involves a great deal of risk.

Part 3 contains just such know-how and horse sense in that it explains the professional method of making a backer's book, whereby you can back several horses in the same race and still show a good profit – the bookmaker's own system in reverse and the staking system used by most of the great gamblers of yesteryear. Their betting exploits, involving astronomical sums of money, have passed into racing history and become legend.

The old-time professionals often backed two or three, or even more, against the field and today some of their heirs still do, but the professional is willing to bet at odds-on to large sums in a way that the average punter would not contemplate. Yet you can still cash in on the professionals' system in handicaps where the odds take a wide range and good prices are the rule rather than the exception. Betting ante-post a day or two before a big handicap in particular, when running plans are largely determined and generally known, may be an especially profitable strategy. Shrewd punters can get the best of the odds about their fancies and reap a handsome reward if they are successful. Exactly how to achieve this desirable goal, based on the skilful use of betting mathematics derived from percentage probability, is fully outlined in the third part of the book.

Our betting manual concludes with a complete guide to the racecourses of Britain, both on the Flat and over jumps. The Racecourse Guide's course descriptions may help you to pick out horses more suited to that particular track or eliminate those which are not likely to run at their best. The effect of the draw is vital in racing. Course modifications, together with new drainage systems have changed much that is familiar in this sphere recently, making some of the old ideas about the draw invalid in many cases. The Racecourse Guide brings you right up-to-date.

The fate of favourites, trainer tips and a special course classification as a benchmark for conclusions about class, essential to the form reader, are other features which make Part 4 a uniquely helpful guide to betting at a particular course.

Most people follow racing for enjoyment but it is my experience that the pleasure is greatly increased when they manage to make a profit. If you have always lost in the past, then try this book. You will find it interesting to read and you may even be in the happy position of having the bookmaker pay for your pastime.

PART 1

How to Pick Winners

Introduction

The pages that follow contain a detailed form guide to most aspects of modern racing embodying a highly focused philosophy of betting. At the heart of this philosophy is the idea of matching method to a particular type of race.

Anyone who thinks at all deeply about the problems associated with backing horses must surely come to the conclusion that there can never be a single master system or betting technique which will deal successfully with all races in all conditions. There are just too many variables in the sport.

The influence of some factors in racing remains constant. The relative fitness of horses and the state of the going are two obvious ones of major importance which are relevant in every sort of race, but what is vital for successful betting is to have a set of logical and workable approaches which look at individual horses against the background of the different kinds and class of event in which they compete. In terms of selection at least, racing on any one day or at a single meeting should not be viewed as a complete whole therefore, but as a composite of separate and distinct entities, each one requiring particularised analysis according to type.

The opening section of this betting manual is not an automatic racing system, but a comprehensive set of guidelines and criteria designed to help negotiate the perils of betting on all kinds of horses in all kinds of races at all kinds of meetings. Individual experience and preference will determine which of the methods is preferred and used most often.

The form guide that follows is not selective, as the backer must be in order to win. Since it is intended to appeal to as wide a readership as possible, it aims to assist its audience in winner-finding across the whole spectrum of racing. It is, however, only a starting point, a launch pad for a new betting career in which hopefully profits will play a prominent part. The specialisation which ought to follow should go far beyond the guidelines, although in some respects the other parts of the book will help to put flesh on the bare bones of the methods of form-assessment explained first. Practice and the flair which may come from experience are needed to complete the process.

Flat (Turf)

The various methodologies featured in this section of Part 1 apply to Flat racing in Britain and are primarily intended for racing on grass. The other code of Flat racing in this country, consisting of all-weather racing at three courses, is so different to the traditional Turf scene that it really calls for a separate treatment in a place other than the present one. For the sake of completeness, however, the Racecourse Guide in Part 4 does contain indicators for the fibresand and equitrack meetings. Also, because the principles of handicapping are always the same, the alternative handicapping method which precedes the criteria for individual types of races can be used for all-weather racing with roughly equal prospects of success.

1
HANDICAPS V. NON-HANDICAPS

The basic distinction for betting purposes, both in regard to selection and arguably staking as well, is between handicaps and those races where differences in weight do not depend on the view of current racing ability taken by the official handicapper. In fact, in only a minority of races in Britain do horses start on absolutely equal terms – even some Classic races, the purest of all tests of the thoroughbred, have an allowance for sex.

There is, however, a world of difference between races where every horse has been given a theoretically identical chance of winning and conditions races where small penalties for previous successes and allowances for age and sex, do not really detract from the goal of establishing the best horse in the race by merit alone. The difference between handicaps and non-handicaps is a very real one and we will begin our analysis by looking at form in the former.

2
Private Handicaps

A handicap race can be a complex problem, and the degree of complexity will depend on the amount of direct and collateral form 'in the book' which is relevant to it. In general, the more form lines that are available, the more complex the problem. Yet the opposite scenario is even worse from the backer's point of view.

A race where the contestants cannot be compared at all by their previous runs against each other, or through the performances of the equine equivalent of third parties, presents an even greater puzzle than one where comparative form is plentiful.

In practice most handicaps fall somewhere between the two extremes. Thus there will be a double difficulty – too much direct and collateral form for some runners and none at all for others. Bridging the gap between the two opposites can sometimes call for skill bordering on psychic intuition that few of us possess.

One way of solving the problem for the average punter is simply to ignore it, or at least to deliberately chose not to become embroiled in the intricacies of weight and distance built up from a multiple of previous races. After all, there are a number of private handicaps available from specialist firms and most newspapers feature the same thing in the form of race ratings. Experts such as 'Postmark' of the *Racing Post* and 'Formcast' of the *Daily Mail*, do the job of unravelling the form conundrum for us. It is perfectly possible to get by as a racing enthusiast without going further into handicaps than studying a set of published ratings in conjunction with all those other winner-finding aids which are readily available to the betting public nowadays in the racing and national press.

If one feels that it would be impossible to better the efforts of expert journalists, it is still advisable to study closely the principles set out in the ensuing pages, although there is no compulsion to apply them as a matter of course to actual races. Even so, from the knowledge and expertise that will hopefully be acquired, it may be possible from time to time to make vital decisions on which cash depends.

If by contrast, one prefers to make an analysis of handicaps and consequently the selections independently, then what follows in the section on 'instant' handicapping, accompanied by the notes on the various aspects of particular types of race, is definitely for you the reader.

3
OVERALL V. VERY RECENT FORM

In the main, although consideration is usually given to very recent races depending on the predilections of the individual private handicapper, race ratings arrive at their assessment of each horse's chance by a continuous study of overall ability in relation to other horses running in, approximately, the same class and over a similar distance. The figure which appears by the name of each horse strongly reflects this fact. This can sometimes mean therefore that where a horse is regarded as 'well in' at the weights the conclusion has been drawn from a piece of form which is weeks, perhaps even months old, even though some slight modification has been made for its latest running.

The relevance of old form like this can only be proved in the race but it should not be forgotten that if a horse is shown as 'well in' with a very high figure, this is a comparison based on a difference of opinion with the official handicap ratings which determined the weight horses have to carry in the first place.

Who gets it right more often? The private handicapper who contrives to have one horse in the ratings a pound or two in hand of the rest of the field, or the official handicapper whose job it is to give a horse in good form just enough weight to allow it to run a series of sound races in its class without actually winning too often.

Private handicaps have their successes but it is the view of this author that backers intending to put down hard cash should always check the last-time-out performance of each runner, whatever significance they attach to newspaper ratings. This is essential, for the fact of the matter is that in a very high percentage of cases a horse's most recent run will give a pretty fair indication of whether or not it is up to winning.

4
Weight and Grade

In examining a horse's most recent racecourse run it is not just a matter of assessing performance on that occasion in relation to the weight it carried compared with the weight it is set to carry now. Everything has to be placed in the context of the grade of the races involved in the comparison.

In this respect 7 lb should be seen as a key amount of weight. There are exceptions to just about everything in racing but, as a working rule, it is a fair proposition that the winner of a handicap is unlikely to prove capable of winning again next time out if the weight it is set to carry represents an increase of more than 7 lb in its official rating. There are instances every season of horses raised as much as 10 or 12 lb in the weights repeating a handicap victory. Nevertheless, the case of an animal improving beyond all recognition is just one of those exceptions we must live with. The form reader has no way of anticipating such an improvement.

On the other hand there are plenty of horses which fail to overcome an increase of only 2–3 lb in their official rating, although in the majority of cases here failure will probably not be solely due to an increase in weight of that order but to any one of several other factors which prevent a horse reproducing its form, i.e. fitness within the form cycle (see Criterion 13), the going (Criterion 14), the draw (Criterion 15), and so on.

But whatever the adjustment in weight, grade stands out as the most important factor of all most of the time when trying to assess form from race to race.

Here too seven is the vital number, for in the author's system each grade in the structure of modern racing is equivalent to 7 lb. This can be seen in the following table:

Group One and Two	+21 lb
Group Three	+14 lb
Listed	+7 lb
Grade A Handicap	10–0
Grade B Handicap	9–7
Grade C Handicap	9–0

Grade D Handicap	8–7
Grade E Handicap	8–0
Grade F Handicap	7–7
Grade G Handicap	7–0

This table represents a personal view of the realities of the situation. The official handicap scale is 65 (G), 70 (F), 75 (E), 90 (D), 100 (C), 110 (B), 115 (A), with no horse rated above 115 allowed to run in a handicap. Other scales are possible. It is all a matter of opinion, but in contrast to the official classification, the scale shown above has the merit of dividing the grades into equal divisions of weight and has been found to work out well in practice.

In any sensible scale there is always a huge weight difference between a horse of the highest class habitually running in Group 1 and one of the lowest racing ability. The difference on the above scale is 4½ st. Some people may even express surprise that the gulf is so wide. Yet there are authorities in racing who assert that a Derby winner could give a selling handicapper 5 st or more and still beat it. If such a race could be arranged it would be a fascinating one for the form expert and might settle a few arguments!

Be that as it may, what is meant in the table is not that the top weight in say, a Class D handicap should carry 8–7. The table is for comparative purposes only, and it is the numerical relationship between the grades that is important. For example, a horse carrying top weight in a D handicap will be roughly 21 lb inferior to one similarly burdened in an A handicap. Or put another way, the general class of horses competing in D races will be approximately 21 lb lower than that of the runners in an A handicap.

Therefore, an increase or decrease in a horse's official rating should not be seen in isolation. It has to be related to race grade. A winner last time out carrying up to 7 lb extra on its reappearance has a reasonable chance of success if it is running in the same grade as before. But, if it is down to run in a race of one grade higher it must find approximately another 7 lb of improvement if it is to succeed. In all it has a 14 lb harder task than it had in its previous race. If it is raised two grades, which is not unusual, it is being asked in real terms to shoulder 21 lb more than last time – 7 lb for the increase in its official handicap rating, and 14 lb (7 lb + 7 lb) for the two rises in class.

No wonder so much money is wasted by unskilled punters who see as the sole justification for a bet, just a '1' against a horse's name, indicating a win last time out for an animal now running off an apparently good weight, whose real severity as a burden is not tested by any sound means. The horse might only be carrying '8 st something', but that weight could actually represent a much stiffer task in weight and grade.

Conversely, a winner last time out up 7 lb in the official ratings but dropped one grade is in fact racing on the same terms as before. If it reproduces its previous form, it has every chance of winning again.

Sometimes a horse is lowered two grades. Remember, the horse's connections, not the Jockey Club handicapper, determine the class of race they run their horse in. Therefore, from time to time, if winning alone and not prize money is their goal, connections may think they have found a golden opportunity for their horse. If the horse is holding its form and has not deteriorated, it has an excellent chance in the lower grade provided that it has not been penalised by too great a rise in its official handicap mark.

5
PLACED HORSES

Obviously, when carrying out a survey of the most recent form in any race that is under review, it is also necessary to consider horses which did not win last time out. Although a horse which ran a very good second will sometimes be raised a pound or two by the handicapper, much to the chagrin of its trainer no doubt, here for the most part we are dealing with horses whose rating remains the same or which is lowered as a result of a poor performance.

In the latter case, however, the reduction is nearly always slight. Whereas a winner of a handicap may be lifted by quite a large amount of weight in a single increase, horses which keep failing to win are moved down the ratings very gradually a pound or two at a time. Therefore a single drop in the weights between races is seldom decisive.

A factor of greater significance which the form reader will frequently have to assess is just how much value should be put on a run where a horse was placed last time out. Again, what significance should be attached to a very poor run when a horse was right down the field?

There have to be extenuating circumstances for a horse which runs pounds below its true form, but it will generally be best to play safe. Taking the view that the horse has quite simply lost its form and the run should be dismissed out of hand will be right more often than it is wrong. The extenuating circumstances need to be pretty compelling to give such a horse a real chance in its next race. Most handicaps are won by horses with sound win-or-place form, or at least which were not beaten far in their previous race. Winners outside this group, with nothing else in their favour, do pop up from time to time, but they fall within the 'impossible' category that the form reader has no alternative but to exclude from his calculations.

For placed horses, however, there is a scale which will measure fairly accurately the distance behind the winner in weight terms. If the weights actually carried by the winner and placed horses are also adjusted by the number of pounds above or below some fixed point, say, 9 st, an exact order of merit revealing by how much weight some horses are superior to others and inferior (or equal) to the rest can easily be constructed.

This is the scale:

Over 5f/6f	1 length = 3 lb
Over 7f	1 length = 2½ lb
From 1m to 1m 3f	1 length = 2 lb
From 1m 4f plus	1 length = 1 lb

Again, the scale is unofficial, but except for one important consideration will be found to be extremely accurate in assessing how placed and close-up horses stand in relation to the winner and each other.

In any finish where there is daylight between the winner and the second the tendency in many races is for jockeys to ease even horses immediately behind the front two if they have no chance of actually winning. This is, strictly speaking, contrary to the rules of racing, at least if the final placings of animals prominent in the finish of a race are thereby affected. Yet despite the vocal disapproval of each-way backers frequently expressed from the stands, regrettably this is accepted practice on our racecourses and for the most part the stewards turn a blind eye to the breach of the rules.

The problem from the point of view of the form reader is that if full value is given to the distance between second and third, and the distances beyond, the inferiority of beaten horses is often exaggerated. Therefore, give full value only to the finishing distance between winner and second, however great the margin, but halve the distances after that when applying the scale to convert to weight.

Also, although the scale accurately assesses the form difference between winners and runners-up, wide-margin winners last time out do not produce as many winners as those which have won by a narrow margin. Whereas the former have probably had the race run to suit them, the latter have shown battling qualities to get home in front. Tough horses like these with the willingness to fight for the lead are often better betting propositions than facile winners who won unchallenged last time out. This statistical fact is in stark contrast to what many punters believe. The practice, followed by many, of going through the card in search of wide-margin winners is in fact a faulty betting strategy.

CONCLUSION

The first stage in analysing handicaps is now complete. Last-time-out form should always be the best guide. If one is not prepared to look at the most recent form of every horse in the race, one should at least examine with a critical eye the most recent run of any horse which is a probable bet. Or, if the field has been narrowed down to a shortlist of possibles by whatever means, a comparison of the previous outings of each candidate ought to be the final arbiter.

By and large the reader coming to handicapping for the first time will do well to take very recent form at its face value and, even for a sophisticated form enthusiast of long standing, tunnel vision of this kind is no bad thing. Our basic methodology has the advantage of processing vital information reasonably quickly and efficiently; excursions into the forest of races beyond the most recent should be kept to a minimum, however adept readers believe themselves to be at interpreting the vagaries of old or hidden form.

6
Instant Handicapping

Last-time-out form in relation to weight and grade should be the main focus of the conventional form reader, possibly combined with an appreciation of the longer view of each horse's chance reflected in race ratings based on a private handicap. Look for very good recent form *and* a high, if not the highest, race rating.

An alternative approach is possible, however. It is based on general, statistical data drawn from the form book and has the advantage of finding favoured horses quickly and automatically, without the backer having to judge the niceties of form. Unique to this book, it has been given the name of 'instant handicapping'.

Instant handicapping is not some miraculous oracle. It will not pick the winner of every handicap. If every single horse indicated by it were backed to win it would probably not produce a level-stakes profit over an extended period, but what it will do is show readers how to choose a great many winners of handicap races, probably a lot more than they have ever been able to pick before.

The method is based on a basic racing truth: class tells in handicaps as much as in any other horse race. Or, horses near the top of the weights win much more often than those at the bottom. This trend is so pronounced that with the aid of a few simple rules it can be converted into a point at which bookmakers, for all their careful regulation of the odds, may be vulnerable.

Instant handicapping was developed many years ago by the author from a large amount of data which is, inevitably, now dated but which has served him well ever since. For the purposes of this book however, and as a way of reaffirming the statistical validity of the principles behind the method, another much smaller survey has been undertaken in which the results of 100 Flat handicaps were recorded before being arranged into a meaningful pattern.

May was chosen for the survey. The new Flat season is about five weeks old at the beginning of the month and form has settled down to a great extent. Trainers are still keen to get races into every one of their charges and fields are definitely large compared with later in the year. This is the ideal scenario for demonstrating the ideas which underpin our instant-handicapping methodology.

The point about the sample of handicap winners set out below is that it is purely random. Once the process of recording results on a daily basis was begun, no winner was omitted, whatever its price or position in the handicap, until the 100-race mark was reached.

The largest field in the block of results was one of 29 runners, and the smallest six, but the vast majority of the 100 races had more than ten runners, often many more. Because in many of the handicaps one or more horses are set to carry an identical weight, it was convenient to assign the positions in the handicap a letter rather than a number – thus avoiding the confusing use of equals signs – where A is always the top weight, B the second horse down in the weights, C the third, and so on. Overweight and the allowance for apprentice jockeys were completely ignored.

SURVEY OF 100 FLAT HANDICAPS

A 4–1 6–1 7–1 8–1 10–1 16–1

B 9–4 4–1 11–2 7–1

C 5–2 5–1 13–2 13–2 7–1 15–2 10–1 12–1 12–1 16–1

D 6–4 100–30 4–1 9–2 9–2 5–1 6–1 6–1 6–1 13–2 13–2 10–1 12–1 12–1 12–1 14–1

E 3–1 9–2 6–1 13–2 7–1 12–1 14–1

F 6–4 9–2 9–2 11–2 9–1 12–1 16–1

G 13–8 7–1 14–1

H 5–2 3–1 4–1 6–1 11–1 16–1

I 5–2 11–4 5–1 9–1 25–1

J 6–1 7–1 14–1

K 4–1 5–1 13–2 10–1 14–1 16–1 25–1

L 11–2 14–1 33–1

M 2–1 7–1 10–1 11–1 16–1 16–1 20–1

N 11–2 15–2

O 6–1 13–2 12–1 20–1 20–1 20–1 33–1

P 8–1

Q 15–8 3–1 7–1

R 11–2

S —

T —

U 16–1

V —

W 12–1

The preceding table reveals some highly significant points which ought to be the subject of further analysis. The quite high number of wins recorded by K, M and in particular by O, where some big prices would have yielded a good level-stakes profit, are almost certainly something of an aberration, and would probably not be repeated in another survey. More likely some other letter or letters would have an exceptional run of good fortune but, although the sample of 100 races is small enough to allow for this kind of luck to play a part, nevertheless there is a clear, and to some extent predictable, pattern in the figure as a whole.

If the general proposition that high weights in handicaps do best and bottom weights do worse is correct and that the weights in between win in approximate proportion to that model, then what you would expect to see is a triangle. With the exception of the two top weights, that is what you have. Looking at the figure from the bottom up and from left to right, the hypotenuse of the triangle can be drawn in from the 12–1 of W to the 14–1 of D.

There is a very good reason to explain why the top two positions have done relatively badly. The handicapper who, according to the most uncharitable view never forgets, tends to be hard on horses which show an exceptional run of form or even run just one exceptional race. Such horses rise rapidly to the head of the weights within their class. Their measure is taken and they are no longer capable of winning off their high rating. Once this has happened, a horse might remain too high in the weights for the rest of its racing career.

This is not an exceptional scenario. It is a situation which, to a greater or lesser degree, occurs all the time and certainly to the extent that any method of betting in handicaps needs to have built into it some device by which animals so afflicted are identified and excluded for betting purposes.

Leaving refinements apart for the moment, it is clear from the figure that the four positions C to F are the best consecutive positions and it is around this area that the vulnerable point for the bookmaker occurs. If there had been an equal distribution of recorded victories, the strike rate for weights would have been $100 \times 4/23 = 17.39$ per cent. The actual strike rate for the positions C to F is in fact much higher, at 40 per cent of the sample.

The author knows from other data, however, that there may be some element of lucky aberration in the F position. Since our final methodology will not abandon the highest weights entirely, it is also worth noting that the five weights A to E produced a total of 43 per cent of the wins. Put another way, over two-fifths of all the handicaps in the survey were won by one of the top five in the weights.

It is also possible to draw some pretty definite, general conclusions about the starting prices of winners. Below are the 100 results arranged according to this factor, where the data has been put into bands of starting prices reflecting various levels of confidence within the racecourse betting market. Once again there appears to be an area where the bookmaker looks vulnerable to the backer who works from statistical record.

Up to 2–1	5 winners
9–4 to 4–1	14 winners
9–2 to 15–2	39 winners
8–1 to 10–1	9 winners
11–1 to 14–1	17 winners
16–1 to 20–1	12 winners
22–1 or over	4 winners

The price range of 9–2 to 15–2 is outstanding with 39 per cent of all winners contained within it. The ranges 9–4 to 4–1 and 11–1 to 14–1 are roughly equal and both produce slightly more winners than 8–1 to 10–1. But, when it comes to choosing a favoured group of prices on which to concentrate, the very narrow 8–1 to 10–1 band added to 9–2 to 15–2 is surely best for the punter.

Horses quoted 9–4 to 4–1 do not offer value in terms of likely profitability from a by no means exceptional strike rate of winners, and 11–1 to 14–1 chances, though clearly more remunerative, are nonetheless much more plentiful which would reduce the overall profitability from successes. Also, they are impossible to identify from newspaper betting forecasts, since they are usually included among the unspecified 'others'.

On the other hand an unbroken price band from 9–2 right up to 10–1 inclusive offers the punter a readily identifiable group of horses from within the normal betting-forecast range. Even if on occasion some of them start and win at longer odds than 10–1 they would still fall into our net. The survey, derived solely from starting prices, showed a strike rate of 48 per cent from the 9–2 to 10–1 band, or nearly half the races. This is definitely the odds range which should be the focus of the punter's attack on the bookmaker.

RULES

We are now in a position to justify the rules of the instant handicapping method which are as follows:

1   Concentrate on the top five horses in the handicap, including all horses set to carry equal fifth weight. Ignore apprentice allowances.
2   Strike out, however, any horse due to be ridden by a jockey claiming either seven or five pounds.
3   Rate the form figures of the two top weights in the race by these scales:

   Six-figure form
   – winner in last three races: 2 pts per win
   – winner in previous three: 1 pt per win
   – placed (2, 3, 4) in any race: 1 pt each place.

   Five-figure form or less
   – winner last time out: 3 pts
   – winner in previous races: 2 pts per win
   – placed (2, 3, 4) in any race: 1 pt each place.

   Strike out any horse with a total of less than 4 points from six-figure form, less than 3 points if it has only run five times in all, or less than 2 points if it has run four times or less.
4   Consider only horses quoted between 9–2 and 10–1 inclusive in the betting forecast of the newspaper you use for betting purposes.

Rule 3 imposes a minimum form qualification in order to eliminate those top-weighted no-hopers of which the handicapper has probably taken full measure, as well as those which find themselves at the top end of the handicap for technical reasons which have nothing to do with racing ability, such as failure to meet qualifying standards for a realistic weight.

Rule 2 eliminates horses ridden by very inexperienced apprentices. They are seldom value for the weight concession. Horses so ridden rarely win, for the presence of a 'chalk' jockey in the plate of a highly weighted runner is in fact a sure sign that a horse is 'not off' today.

It was gratifying to find that although there had been a considerable gap in time since the rules of instant handicapping were originally formulated, the survey of a block of recent results did not call for any modification in the rules. The instant handicapping method appears as good now as when it was created.

How often can you expect to win with it? We have already admitted that it is not a magic oracle, but the punter who turns to it as a selection method still has every right to expect some very good days.

Take for example Thursday, 25 May in the year in which I write. There were two meetings that day and three handicaps at each meeting. The complete 'instant' record was as follows:

GOODWOOD

3.10   7f   Class C

09100–0	CHAMPAGNE RIDER	Form count: 1.	Eliminated
0–01852	MISTER RAMBO	Form count: 2.	Eliminated
6/7035–6	CHEWIT	L. Newman (5).	Eliminated
090–244	PRINCE BABAR	7–1.	Selected
200–066	BOOMERANG BLADE	Not 9–2 to 10–1.	Eliminated

Probable SP: 6 Peartree House, 7 Hyperactive, Prince Babar, 8 Bintang Timor, Karameg, Mister Rambo, 10 Second Wind, 11 Elmhurst Boy, 12 Amber Fort, Chewit, Welcome Gift.

Selection: Prince Babar

Result: Gift of Gold (9th in the weights) Won 25–1
Prince Babar 5th 7–1

3.40   1m 6f   Class B

00133–4	SALMON LADDER	Form count: 4, but not 9–2 to 10–1.	Eliminated
320–224	MURGHEM	Form count: 5, but not 9–2 to 10–1.	Eliminated
11200–9	PAIRUMANI STAR	10–1.	Selected
145320–	MONTALCINO	Not 9–2 to 10–1.	Eliminated
7000–07	TURTLE VALLEY	Not 9–2 to 10–1.	Eliminated

Probable SP: 9–2 Afterjacko, 5 Little Pippin, 6 Zilarator, 7 Livius, Montechristo, 8 Tensile, 10 Pairumani Star, 12 Murghem, Salmon Ladder, Turtle Valley, 14 Quedex.

Selection: Pairumani Star

Result: Pairumani Star Won 12–1

5.20   5f   Class E   Apprentice race

760–206	FORGOTTEN TIMES	Form count: 1.	Eliminated
366154	BEWARE	Form count: 4. 7–1.	Selected
1246–00	ECUDAMAH	8–1.	Selected
00000–0	SIHAFI	7–1.	Selected
000–000	POLAR MIST	10–1.	Selected

Probable SP: 4 Beyond The Clouds, 5 Forgotten Times, 7 Beware, Sihafi, Nightingale Song, 8 Ecudamah, 10 Polar Mist, Dancing Lily, Half Tone.

Selections: Beware, Ecudamah, Sihafi, Polar Mist

Result: Polar Mist Won 12–1
Sihafi 4th 9–1
Beware 5th 11–2
Educamah 9th 15–2

NEWCASTLE

3.20   1m   Class E

114423	SIGN OF THE TIGER	Form count: 6. F. Goode (3) 5–1.	Selected
43167–0	TOP OF THE CLASS	Form count: 3.	Eliminated
7–88	HAIKAL	Not 9–2 to 10–1.	Eliminated
662440	DONTBESOBOLD	Not 9–2 to 10–1.	Eliminated
619–00	MARVEL	Not 9–2 to 10–1.	Eliminated

Probable SP: 9–4 Mister Clinton, 5 Sign Of The Tiger, 7 Alpathar, 8 One Domino, Nowt Flash, 10 Top Of The Class, Flying Carpet, 12 Watergold.

Selection: Sign Of The Tiger

Result: Sign Of The Tiger Won 6–1

3.50   2m   Class D

111112–	VIRGIN SOLDIER	Form count: 8. 6–1.	Selected
41–6	FREETOWN	Form count: 3. 11–2.	Selected
790708–	PASS THE REST	Not 9–2 to 10–1.	Eliminated
17–6000	YES KEEMO SABEE	Not 9–2 to 10–1.	Eliminated
418–890	GIVE AN INCH	Not 9–2 to 10–1.	Eliminated

Probable SP: 7–2 Generous Ways, 5 Kagoshima, 11–2 Freetown, 6 Virgin Soldier, 7 Legendry Line, Old Hush Wing, 10 Sposa, Northern Motto.

Selections: Virgin Soldier, Freetown

Result: Virgin Soldier Won 10–1
Freetown 2nd 3–1

4.20   5f   Class E

187–0	CAUTIOUS JOE	Form count: 2. B. McHugh(7).	Eliminated
885787	AVONDALE GIRL	Form count: 0.	Eliminated
634–36	DAWN	R. Cody-Boutcher(7).	Eliminated
250–960	TWICKERS	8–1.	Selected
101600	FRILLY FRONT	7–1.	Selected

Probable SP: 6 Naissant, 7 Frilly Front, Bollin Ann, 8 Twickers, Record Time, 10 Dawn, Angel Hill, 12 High Carry, Tancred Times.

Selections: Twickers, Frilly Front

Result: Bollin Ann (6th in the weights) Won 6–1
Twickers unplaced 12–1
Frilly Front unplaced 10–1

Thus the following successes and failures emerged for the day:

> Loser in one pick
> 12–1 winner in one pick
> 12–1 winner in four picks
> 6–1 winner in one pick
> 10–1 winner in two picks
> Two losers in two picks.

It would be wrong to expect such a spectacular return too often. The examples do demonstrate, however, the very real potential of the method in a difficult area of racing speculation.

Several horses are often indicated in the same race. This is unavoidable and it is left to the reader to decide exactly how to use the instant handicapping method. You might make a choice based on your reading of form or you may prefer simply not to bet when the method indicates more than one horse. Or again, you might decide to back all the possibles in a race, dividing the stakes equally or regulating stakes more systematically as explained in Part 3.

At all events instant handicapping is a viable alternative to conventional ways of assessing form in handicaps. Selections are fully automatic, no judgement is required on the part of the punter, and it is the work of a few minutes to check out the daily indications. If attracted to the method, one has every chance of finding many winners in the future.

On the other hand, we have said that specialisation pays the biggest dividends, and there now follows a series of criteria in which very specific guidelines are given for various types of race.

7
CRITERION 1 – FIVE-FURLONG SPRINT HANDICAPS

Even more than with handicaps in general, sprint handicaps over the minimum trip are usually won by horses near the top of the weights which are also well to the fore in the betting.

1 Concentrate on the top half dozen in the weights (slightly more in very big fields).

2 Concentrate on a similar number of horses at the head of the betting.

3 Winners last time out frequently win again. But even over this minimum trip where weight might be thought to have less effect, an increase of more than seven pounds in the ratings may well be enough to prevent a repeat victory.

4 Horses which have been running well without winning or even being placed can and do win sprints. Here form from some time ago can suddenly become indicative of a probable win, although the horse has been just short of concert pitch in very recent outings. The market on the race compared with the betting forecast often provides the clue that a sprinter is 'off' today.

5 Five furlongs is a specialist distance both for horses and trainers. Never ignore lightly the chance of a runner trained by one of the small number of handlers who specialise in winning sprint handicaps. They have purple patches from time to time in these races when every runner from the stable suddenly improves by leaps and bounds. They even win with 'cast-offs' from other stables.

   Currently, D. Nicholls, A. Berry, J. Glover and P. Makin are the trainers who lead in this area. One of the 'secrets' of the success of trainers who target sprints is that they focus on making a horse quick from the stalls. Speed at the gate is usually the difference between winning and losing in these races.

8
CRITERION 2 – SIX-FURLONG HANDICAPS

These events are not the object of specialisation to the same extent as races over the minimum distance. However, more than in the latter, the key here is winning form over the trip, although not necessarily last time out.

Therefore:

1 Consider only horses which won last time out or which have won at least one of their last three runs or which have won at least two of their last six runs.

   This rule will have a severe 'pruning' effect in many races, but strict adherence to it will pay off over time.

2 Ignore horses in the bottom third of the weights.

3 Provided a horse is not hopelessly overburdened by being put up a huge amount in the weights as a penalty for a facile win, ignore the study of weight. It may not help much in six-furlong handicaps.

4 Even races of this type with enormous fields are seldom won by a horse priced over 16–1. The betting market on the course is far and away the best indicator for the shrewd punter who can spot when money is 'talking'.

9
Criterion 3 – Two-mile Plus Handicaps

There are not a lot of these races but horses at or near the top of the handicap are much the best. Class tells over a distance of ground. Therefore:

1 Concentrate on the top third of the handicap.

2 Consider say, only the first five in the betting in races of 16 or more runners, and roughly *pro rata* for races with fewer contestants.

3 Look for horses which are ultra consistent as revealed in the six-figure form summary. It is not necessary to insist on a preponderance of winning over placed form, but too many '0's in the form line make a staying handicapper a suspect betting proposition.

10
Criterion 4 – Form Figures in All Handicaps

It is possible for a backer to find winners of handicaps consistently by simply studying the three-figure form lines of the runners, either in conjunction with other factors or even in isolation. The merit of this approach is that not many handicappers actually record the most favoured figures.

The sequences established as those producing most winners in handicaps, after a large amount of research are, in approximate order of merit:

Top Rank	101 131 011 112
Second Rank	321 311 121 122
Third Rank	111 211 114
Handicaps for 3-y-os only and nurseries	11 21

11
CRITERION 5 – MAIDEN WINNERS FIRST TIME IN A HANDICAP

Horses, three-year-olds for the most part, which have won a maiden race and which are now running in a handicap race for the first time, have a poor record. They hardly ever go on to win a good class handicap (A to C) immediately and are suspect propositions in races of lesser class.

Maiden-race winners made favourite to win their first run in a handicap are especially poor value as a betting medium. Some of them, running in big handicaps and trained by a fashionable trainer are sometimes at very short odds. They hardly ever win but punters are 'taken in' in droves time after time. The Newmarket trainer L. Cumani, however, is one leading handler who is something of the exception who proves the rule.

12
CRITERION 6 – NURSERIES

The days when nurseries, that is handicaps for two-year-olds, were the medium of betting coups by clever stables have long gone. Nevertheless, the market related to very simple form study is a fair guide and these events are by no means as formidable as races for older horses.

1   The first four in the betting are heavily favoured (first five in fields of 16 or more runners).

2   As a general form prescription, winners last time out are to be preferred to seconds in their previous race which in turn are better than thirds and fourths.

3   Unlike three-year-olds, many two-year-old maiden winners go on to score in a nursery handicap at the first time of asking but, be wary of the winners of sellers. However low their weight, the rise in class will nearly always put paid to their chance.

13
Non-Handicaps – Backing and Opposing Favourites

Although it is a view that has been challenged in some quarters in recent years, traditional racing wisdom holds that the backer's best chance lies in trying to find the winners of non-handicaps and that those races in which the handicapper has an influence should be avoided by the serious punter. It is a fact in support of this view for instance that both on the Flat (turf) and over jumps (hurdles and chases) approaching 80 per cent of all winners in stakes races emanate from the first three in the betting forecast. On the other hand handicaps, judged either from the point of view of betting forecasts or the actual market on races, are nothing like so consistent. No category of handicap under any code of racing can boast the same kind of statistic.

However, even if a non-handicap race can be narrowed down to just three possibles much of the time, which one of three will actually win remains a major conundrum. Also, the odds available for 'live' candidates in non-handicaps are on the whole some way below the rate of return for fancied runners in handicaps.

In all except the most competitive conditions races, given the expertise of both bookmakers and backers in reading form, *the favourite should win,* but will rarely be at a generous price. If the backer opts for a horse which is not favourite, even though it is second or third favourite, this generally means that the indications of form are being ignored.

The secret of winning in this area of betting, as in all others, is to find enough winners at prices good enough to ensure an overall profit. In practice finding the right blend of first, second and third favourites is a feat beyond most punters.

As a starting point to solving this perennial problem, the following question should be to the fore of the reader's mind every time a non-handicap race is considered as a potential betting proposition:

**If the favourite is, theoretically, the best horse in
the race at the weights, but only 35 per cent or so**

of all favourites actually win nowadays, is the
favourite in the race under review one that is
likely to succeed or fail?

It is a simple enough question but one with enormous significance
in determining how the backer should proceed. In this respect
statistics can be a great help, at least if one is comfortable with
statistics in racing to the point where they may sometimes
contradict a personal opinion.

For the purposes of this book, a survey of 500 conditions races
on the Flat was undertaken. Betting-forecast favourites were
arranged by their odds and the number of winners and losers in
each of four price ranges carefully recorded.

The outcome was as follows:

Horses quoted at odds-on in the betting forecast	54.8% won
Horses quoted from evens to 6–4 inclusive	55.6% won
Horses quoted from 13–8 to 11–4 inclusive	26.1% won
Horses quoted at 3–1 or over	9.1% won

There are small but variable profits to be had from random betting
on favourites in the first two categories, although too small
probably to satisfy the ordinary punter wagering in moderate
stakes. Forget about profit and loss for the moment however and
consider only the winning percentages. Surely, for anyone who
backs a lot of horses regularly, the following prescriptions, derived
from the above survey, must make sense.

1 Back all odds-on chances in the betting forecast to win.

2 Back all horses quoted between evens and 6–4 to win.

3 Back some horses quoted at between 13–8 and 11–4 to win, but
   in some races with a betting-forecast favourite in this price
   range, find an alternative selection.

4 Automatically oppose any horse quoted as favourite at 3–1 or
   longer in the betting forecast with some other selection.

I personally see nothing wrong in principle with betting at odds-on but, for the many who do not like laying the odds, the first rule could be amended to read:

When the favourite is odds-on in the betting forecast do not oppose it with a bet on some other selection.

Eyebrows will no doubt be raised in some quarters at such a set of sweeping generalisations which restrict the backer's freedom of action across the board in a number of vital respects when it comes to backing favourites. But, hopefully, readers will grasp the point that is being made, even if they ultimately reject some or all of the prescriptions as automatic betting tactics.

When attending a race meeting with the intention of having a bet on every race, or when going down the day's cards in the morning newspaper with a view to having a bet, it is usual to pick out some favourites and avoid others. Hitherto this process will have been entirely subjective, governed by one's own knowledge, prejudices and preferences.

But, how often is this right? How often does one pick out one 6–4 chance that gets beaten and disregard another horse at the same price which wins? More often than one cares to admit is almost certainly the answer.

Instead of relying on personal judgement of form, suppose we make the above conclusions a set of absolute, inviolable precepts based on statistics, not fallible human judgement. This will then be right more often than not. Perhaps one should not bet on every race at a meeting (although bookmakers do) and be more selective in betting from home, but the general point remains valid.

As a first step in assessing any race the favourite's chance should be examined and action taken accordingly. If punters are prepared to put their faith in statistics, the aforementioned quartet of rules provide an automatic *modus operandi* to guide their betting actions.

Needless to say many will reject such a mechanistic approach. But even the most confident and talented reader of form will find food for thought here, and although not wishing to adopt every one of the four rules as a matter of course, some readers may be prepared to let non-handicap betting be influenced to a greater or lesser extent by them.

Within the main survey of 500 races a number of other possibilities concerning the favourite were considered. The results of this secondary investigation are set out below. Remember that only non-handicap races are within its scope.

Where the betting forecast favourite was at odds against, but was replaced as favourite in the actual racecourse market, 22.7 per cent of the original favourites won.

Since there was a 6.8 per cent level-stakes profit on outlay from backing all horses which met this qualification, the view often touted among some media pundits and others that a favourite which drifts in the market 'cannot win' is simply not true. On balance it is better to back the drifter than to oppose it, certainly unless there is a good and sufficient reason to account for the lack of confidence reflected in the betting market.

Another frequent circumstance surrounding favourites was investigated and the outcome was as follows:

Where the favourite was at odds against in the betting forecast, but was backed down to start at odds-on in the racecourse betting, 55.6 per cent of such favourites actually won.

Unfortunately here things are not quite so clear-cut, for backing all non-handicap favourites which behaved in this manner produced a level-stakes loss of 24.3 per cent overall, despite the high percentage of winners. Clearly there is nothing in this circumstance to help the backer in a positive sense, although an important negative conclusion can be drawn, namely that in statistical terms at least there needs to be a very good reason to bet against the trend and oppose a favourite which shortens up to odds-on in the pre-race betting exchanges.

One other question was asked in assessing the results of the survey. This concerned the fate of betting-forecast favourites quoted at odds-on in the morning newspaper, but which drifted out to odds against on the course, although still remaining clear favourites. The finding in this respect was that there are very few such horses. No clear trend emerged, with about half winning and half losing, but it would be pointless to cite exact figures because the sample was too small for any serious statistical conclusion to be drawn.

It is hoped that this survey is of value. Even if readers are unwilling to act to the letter upon the conclusions which emerged, thereby making them an automatic part of non-handicap betting strategy, at least the realities of the situation are now known in the case of the various betting scenarios discussed. And, in the uncertain world of backing horses, certain knowledge is a precious commodity.

The survey focused on non-handicaps in general, but non-handicaps can be broken down further into a number of different types, far more in fact than is the case with handicaps. This opens up an obvious avenue for specialisation and specialisation is the backer's best chance of winning in the long run. Good recent form, especially last time out, is as always the racing enthusiast's greatest ally and most effective weapon in the struggle with the layers. However, it may pay to apply this guiding principle to one or perhaps just a few of the various kinds of stakes race. Hence the analysis of main categories which follows, although space prevents a full and separate examination of some of the sub-categories, especially those which are grouped together under the heading of 'conditions races' in the guidelines to be found in the next few pages.

14
CRITERION 7 – GROUP ONE/TWO RACES FOR THREE-YEAR-OLDS AND OVER

For betting purposes one of three possible form profiles is generally found in the races which make up the top flight of British racing. There is the very competitive event with plenty of runners. Many have high-class form and there are quite a number of horses which hold a reasonable chance of winning. The Classic races, with the usual exception of the much less competitive St Leger, are invariably of this type. At the other extreme we find races with relatively small fields that have 'cut up' to such an extent that an odds-on favourite, which on all known form should win, apparently dominates proceedings. In races of the third sort, where just two or three horses seem to have a real chance, the punter has a straightforward choice, but knows only too well that it is easy to be on the 'wrong one'.

In the case of the presence of a 'hotpot' or 'good thing' in the field, on balance it is best not to attempt to 'buy money' at very short odds. Odds-on favourites in Group One or Group Two are more reliable than their counterparts further down the racing scale, but they are not infallible, and from time to time they flop to the astonishment of the racing *cognoscenti*. Horses, even horses of the highest class, are not machines.

The better bet is to ignore the presumed 'certainty' and to go for an 'each-way steal' as it is sometimes called. This is a horse with sound form that might just upset the favourite. If such a horse has an outstanding chance of finishing in a place at least equal to the favourite's chance of winning, it will be good business to back it each-way, even though the punter is prepared to accept the loss of the win part of the wager. Once in a while there is a shock result and the backer on the only realistic alternative to the favourite will reap a handsome reward. Even if the favourite wins, its very short price inflates the odds for the rest of the field to an unrealistic level. The each-way better is therefore almost certain to break even, even though the bookmaker will pay only one-fifth the odds for a place, or in the case of some firms, only one-sixth when the favourite in a non-handicap starts at odds-on.

It does not do, however, to oppose every odds-on chance in a big stakes race with each-way bets. The horse chosen for a win-and-place bet should be as outstanding for a place as the favourite apparently is for a win. If the backer can additionally find even a slight chink in the favourite's armour such as doubtful stamina or a tendency to prefer different going, then the each-way steal is truly a 'bet-to-nothing'. For example, the race for the 1999 St Leger threw up precisely such a bet. The odds-on favourite Ramruma had won the Oaks on soft ground but, on both form and breeding, there was a substantial doubt as to whether she would stay the extra distance of the Doncaster race on the very firm ground that prevailed at Town Moor. By contrast Mutafaweq, a Royal Ascot winner on lightning-fast ground, seemed certain to stay every yard of the St Leger trip. The outcome is history. Mutafaweq ran out the winner of a hard-fought contest and rewarded the 'each-way thieves' at a handsome 11–2, while those who had 'laid the odds' on Ramruma lost their cash on a gallant filly that finished an honourable second.

Where one of these races looks very open, it should be remembered that this is the top level of racing and that form still works out well. The favoured form figures cited in Criterion 4 are especially effective as a winner-finding aid in this class of competition although here 111 stands out and the remainder are fairly equal in rank. Conversely, inconsistent animals with poor form figures should be left severely alone. Statistics tell us that it is highly unusual for the winner of such events to be outside the first five in the betting.

Most Group One and Group Two winners are horses with established form at the highest level that have been specifically prepared for their races as part of a career strategy. Therefore the backer should be wary of the type of animal which, on the strength of a single brilliant run, is suddenly asked to break into the highest echelons of competition. This certainly applies in Classic trials in the spring of each year, when fitness gives an advantage to precocious types that cannot be sustained in the big race itself.

Even when connections are prepared to go to the considerable expense of supplementing a horse for a big race, it is generally one of the established stars which succeeds and the newcomer is found to just lack the class necessary to repeat its impressive performance at the lower level. Recently, there have been a couple of exceptions to this trend but, generally speaking, even the top yards often get it wrong in these cases, at least in so far as prize money for a win, though not necessarily a place, is concerned.

Since Classic and other Group One and Two contenders are now trained with the utmost tenderness to ensure that they hold their form, a long absence is no barrier to success in an important stakes race. These days, far more than in the past, the best horses are prepared at home for their long-term objectives, in contrast to lesser animals which are expected to earn their keep on the racecourse by the alternative route of winning a few races from a lot of runs. Participation in actual races at Group level is kept to the minimum compatible with establishing a reputation for stud purposes as much as for gathering prize money. Fitness can therefore be taken on trust in racing's showpiece events.

15
CRITERION 8 – GROUP THREE/LISTED RACES

GROUP THREE RACES

For different reasons a great many Group Three races are just as competitive as the most open Group One event, but form is far more suspect here when it comes to trying to spot winners.

A typical Group Three race might be made up of one or two horses dropped from Group Two (though rarely Group One), horses which habitually compete at this Group Three level and several hopefuls graduating as winners from Listed races or even jumping directly from winning a big handicap to this much tougher grade. Fields are on the medium to small side, but recent form, even last-time-out form, can be extremely difficult to assess in this mixed company. However, the shrewd backer who bears in mind the following points can keep ahead of the game:

1 Horses that have had a number of outings in Group Two but which have never quite succeeded at that level are not likely to fare much better in Group Three. The drop in grade is nearly always more of a warning sign than a recommendation.

2 Listed race winners can and do graduate without too much difficulty to the higher grade. A good win last time out in a Listed event is one of the more reliable indicators of a potential Group Three winner.

3 Very few good handicappers make the grade in Group class, for to do so means they have been seriously underestimated in the early part of their careers. The exception is a lightly raced three-year-old which, by its racecourse performances, has demonstrated that it is improving so quickly that it ought to experience little difficulty in competing against established Group Three performers. Consecutive wins in handicaps is almost invariably the first signpost to success in Group Three for this type of improving three-year-old but, unlike most good winners of Listed races, they are not inevitable winners in Group company. Some make the grade and some do not.

4   The leading stables dominate Group One and Group Two. Group Three is a far more democratic affair. Do not be put off a horse with apparently winning credentials in Group Three just because it is trained at one of the less-fashionable yards.

5   In so far as race distance is concerned, Group Three sprints are far and away the most reliable from a form point of view.

6   Over other distances the betting forecast is frequently a poor guide. Winners start at all kinds of prices. However, paradoxically, actual racecourse favourites are reasonably sound bets. They only win according to the statistical average for all non-handicaps, but starting prices are on the whole well above average. In a race where the form indicators are confused, the market leader is often the best bet. Stakes on these and, indeed, on all horses in Group Three, should be kept on the low side.

LISTED RACES

Listed Race winners are a mixture of improving horses and older animals that have been established for some time at this level. Failed Group Three horses are best avoided.

The improvers are three-year-olds for the most part. They may have arrived by the handicap route or could have done well in conditions races of the better sort, but they are nearly always readily identifiable by their racecourse performances.

Older horses are much more 'in and out'. They tend to win occasionally from a mixture of races in Listed company itself, a few tilts at Group Three and not infrequent pot hunting in Class B or C conditions events. It may well be extremely difficult to tell from the form book when their time to win is due.

However, in medium-sized fields particularly, the betting forecast is a fair guide. More than in Group Three races, the first three in the betting forecast account for the majority of winners but favourites have only an average record, judged by the criterion of profit and loss at level stakes. To bet confidently in Listed races calls for a specialist in this area of competition.

Horses from Listed company dropping into handicaps are not automatic winners. They will receive no concession in the weights from the handicapper and need everything in their favour to succeed.

16
CRITERION 9 – CONDITIONS RACES

This group of races makes up the entire non-handicap racing programme below Listed class. It consists of events actually called 'conditions' races, classified stakes in which only horses whose official rating does not exceed a specified figure may compete, auction races, selling races and those events restricted to apprentice or amateur riders. Maiden races are another large group of non-handicaps and these will be dealt with separately. It is also possible to combine some of two types of race in one, a device which is sometimes employed by racecourse executives to add variety to their cards. For the purposes of betting, the student of form should draw a clear distinction between the relatively small number of races labelled 'conditions' events and the rest.

'Conditions' races are 'open' races, entry for which is not restricted in any of the ways that define the composition of other kinds of non-handicap. They are the best class of non-handicap below Listed events and are graded B to D. Featuring only animals of some ability in the main, form works out extremely well in them. Favourites have an above-average record – in the region of 50 per cent win. Consequently, since they were introduced in 1993, a number of systems exploiting this high percentage of winners with various staking plans have appeared.

The other types of non-handicap are a mixture of events competed for by inferior animals. On the whole, form is unreliable and the backer should proceed carefully. From time to time circumstances throw up a runner with an apparently excellent chance on form that has the appearance of a banker. But starting prices are unlikely to be generous and as with all horses of inferior class, however outstanding in relation to the opposition, reproduction of known form cannot be taken on trust. The added complication of an indifferent ride from an apprentice or amateur jockey adds to the need for caution in those races restricted to this kind of assistance from the saddle.

On the whole, whereas conditions races, especially of classes B and C, are a sound medium for form readers in which to bet, the backer should not habitually bet in non-handicaps below that standard. The risks are too great relative to the possible rewards.

17
CRITERION 10 – MAIDEN RACES

Usually restricted to three-year-olds but occasionally open to older horses as well, almost by definition these races feature animals with unexposed form. Horses that have never run but which may be capable of winning are an additional complicating factor. A measure of caution is therefore needed in maiden races, both in regard to betting in a race itself and to drawing form conclusions for the future from it.

Since a few top yards tend to 'farm' all classes of maiden race by dint of the superior ability of the animals generally at their disposal, the name of the trainer of a runner is usually more important than anything it has accomplished so far on the racecourse. This is particularly true of southern and Newmarket-based raiders operating on northern tracks. Where a horse trained by a top handler has put up at least one promising racecourse performance, there may be a sound case for a good bet. Even on some of the smaller tracks in the north, opinions can take a wide range in maiden events and starting prices for raiders from the most fashionable stables, many of which do not bet, can be worthwhile.

Note also maidens from the big Newmarket stables that are described as 'backward' or 'bit backward' on their initial racecourse run. The chances are that the horse will be a very different proposition next time out and may be something to bet on. Other significant comments in the official form book on the running of maidens are 'scope' or 'good sort'. Again, a horse so labelled from a big yard is almost certainly bound to improve rapidly and put its initial, warm-up run well behind it next time out.

Backers should also be aware of another factor that applies particularly in maiden races. Namely that it is very bad policy to back a maiden filly to beat maiden colts. No filly's form should be taken at face value at least until she has got her head in front at the business end of a race. Even in races confined to fillies, maidens are not generally trustworthy racing machines. Paradoxically, fillies of the very top class are arguably the most reliable of all thoroughbreds on the racecourse, but in maiden races if you never back a filly you will probably be the richer for it in the long run.

18
CRITERION 11 – TWO-YEAR-OLDS

Methods in training juveniles have changed radically in the last 20 years or so. Only genuinely precocious, speedy types which may not have much of a future in their second season are exploited to the full as juveniles. With the remainder the aim is as far as possible to educate them for a three-year-old campaign, with winning at two only a secondary consideration.

This is very bad news for the modern punter, and is reflected in the steep decline in the percentages of winning two-year-old favourites at many courses. Nevertheless a two-year-old with good form, and winning form in particular, is still a sound betting medium if demonstrably superior to its rivals by a comparison of racing records.

A sound system for all two-year-old races is to confine bets to the first three in the betting forecast and to keep to those horses which won or were at least placed last time out. A successful, particular application of this strategy is explained in detail later in this book in the section on systems.

The study of comparative times, based on the principle of comparing the time of a juvenile winner against the standard for the distance with the times recorded by older horses over sprint trips at the same meeting, can also be a fruitful source of future winners.

Two-year-old form nowadays is at its most reliable in August, September and a dry October because all juvenile form is by then largely exposed. Additionally, the better class two-year-olds which have been given plenty of time to come to hand are now on show.

19
CRITERION 12 – CLAIMING RACES

Claiming races or 'claimers' are near the bottom of the scale in terms of the overall racing programme, being ranked only marginally superior to sellers and races for apprentice and amateur riders. Officially non-handicaps, in reality they are a sort of half-way house between handicaps and non-handicaps. Their non-handicap status is confirmed if, as sometimes happens, one or just a small number of horses stand out when the weights are compared with the official ratings for themselves and their rivals. The difference is that in a claimer, trainers nominate the sum of money for which horses can be 'claimed' by someone else, though this right is seldom exercised. This gives the horse a handicap mark and determines the weight to be carried. Hence the divergence with the Jockey Club handicapper's official assessments.

In the US such races and variants of them are much more plentiful, presumably because Americans dislike the power of the official handicapper to influence results, connections preferring to rely on their own estimates of their charges' ability to determine how they are placed in races. Claiming races are contested by horses of most classes, with very good horses sometimes competing for rich purses. The racing culture of the US is very different to that of the UK however.

In this country, claimers were introduced to add interest to the racing scene but, in fact, they are not popular with punters and most trainers. They are invariably contested by poorer quality animals which connections are prepared to risk losing. Quite often there has been some physical or other training difficulty. Most fields for claiming events include a few downright bad horses of selling-plate class. For these reasons it usually pays to follow a simple rule which more often than not will separate out the 'quick' from the 'dead':

Ignore the bottom third of the field in the weights completely and examine most closely the top third.

Horses in the middle of the weights can go either way in terms of the overall class of the race. A study of the official ratings, which are published in the racing press (but not in daily newspapers), may reveal the tendency of the middle zone.

Where a horse that is the 'spot horse' of a published private handicap or of newspaper race ratings also emerges as 'best in' when the weights are compared with the official ratings, it is a runner which, on form, should win. Claimers are usually won by one of the first three in the betting forecast.

20
CRITERION 13 – FITNESS

A vital factor in determining whether a horse can win is its current state of fitness. In a non-handicap a horse's fitness can be more-or-less taken on trust once the season has passed its initial, opening phase. Unraced two-year-olds and three-year-olds which may be given an educational run, are the obvious exceptions. In handicaps, on the other hand, probably no other single factor influences results so much.

The reason is that many horses are raced in handicaps when not at their absolute peak in order to secure a favourable handicap mark that will enable them to succeed when they are finally trained 'to the minute'. Whether a handicapper is 'off' or 'not off' in today's race can sometimes, but by no means always, be inferred from a study of the dates of its races in relation to how they ran in them. Look out for the horse that begins to improve early in the season after a poor run or two.

Similarly once a horse's season is reasonably advanced it may be given a rest at some point to recuperate. Again, look for much improved form following a mid-season lay-off of about a month or slightly more. The horse will have been 'let down' and then gradually brought back to its peak. It could soon be in the winner's enclosure.

A further clue to a horse's readiness to win a handicap can be gained by examining the distances over which it has been running. Every horse has an optimum trip and in the case of all but unexposed three-year-olds, the form book usually provides the necessary information. The official handicapper is probably aware that a horse is not doing itself justice because it is running over a distance either too long or too short for it but the unwritten rules of the game say that the horse should be dropped in the weights after several poor runs. When an animal has had two or three races at the 'wrong' distance and is suddenly put back to its best distance, this can be taken as a strong clue that its trainer is finally satisfied with its handicap rating. Then it becomes a trier with a real chance of winning.

There are other important points about fitness which must be noted by the form reader:

1   Generally speaking, any Flat horse which has not run for about 28 days or more has a slight question mark about its fitness in a handicap.

2   The time lapse that will return a horse fit and well to the racecourse after a rest is related to the distance of the races in which it competes. Sprinters can reappear within a few days with no loss of form. Stayers need much longer to recuperate. Two-year-olds should have a lay-off of at least 10 days if they are not to be damaged.

3   There are exceptions, but horses in general hold their form for no longer than a month. After that some deterioration from the peak of well-being is to be expected. The start of a fresh 'form wave' can sometimes be detected from a close study of the form book, as explained above.

4   A gradual rise in the level of a horse's form is usually more reliable than sudden and spectacular improvement from one race to another.

Be wary of a horse that runs really well after a long absence. It quite often fails to reproduce the form next time out.

In this respect the top trainers make fewer mistakes than their less fashionable counterparts. They have the luxury of time on their side, whereas the average handler is subject to pressures which may prevent him or her from preparing the horse in the best possible way. Connections want to see their horse run and trainers need cash flow, even if it only comes from place money in small races. The result is that horses may be rushed in a way that top yards, with wealthy owners having lots of horses, can avoid.

Even so, any horse coming back with a big run after a long rest is not certain to go on, whoever trains it.

21
CRITERION 14 – THE GOING

Next to fitness, the going preference of individual horses is the single most important factor in determining whether they will show their best form on the racecourse.

A liking for a particular type of going can improve a horse by many pounds. Conversely, dislike of the prevailing ground conditions, if pronounced enough, can ruin a horse's chance of winning a race completely.

Most horses like one type of ground – somewhere between firm and heavy – and dislike the opposite. There are, however, a minority of horses that are equally effective on any going. Good going is neutral in the sense that, whatever their preferences, all horses will run reasonably well on it.

In terms of the conformation of the thoroughbred a few observations here may help the racing enthusiast who combines form with paddock study and race-reading.

A horse with a rounded action, particularly at the forelegs, will most likely have a preference for some give in the ground. Sharp-actioned horses tend to need fast ground. Big, heavy-topped animals will be happiest on softish going because its reduces the pressure on their forelegs. Horses that dislike firm ground tend to dislike running downhill.

The conformation of a racehorse is the study of a lifetime and compressing observations about ground preferences and physical build of a horse into one small paragraph will perhaps have done readers of this book no real favours. Fortunately, however, once a horse has raced a few times, its going predilections can usually be divined from the form book. In the absence of clues from the form record, a horse's breeding is frequently indicative of its preferences, and here it is the sire and not the dam which, nearly always, is the determining influence. In cases of doubt the tables set out in Criterion 16 will provide a fairly accurate indicator of how the state of the ground is likely to affect the offspring of leading sires.

There are three other major points which the backer should keep in mind about the going:

1 Heavy ground generally favours front-running horses.

2 When the ground is fast, favourites and form horses tend to win. When it is soft, form is suspect and heavy conditions usually see more outsiders winning than usual. Therefore wise backers adjust their stakes when extremes of going prevail.

3 Do not put much faith for the future in form achieved on heavy ground, unless there is a long spell of wet weather, as there sometimes is in the autumn.

22
CRITERION 15 – THE EFFECT OF THE DRAW

In all kinds of race up to a distance of a mile, and occasionally even further, the draw has an influence on the outcome of races at some courses, although the degree of influence can vary even on the same course due to the position of the starting stalls, going conditions, jockeys' tactics, and so on. On a small number of courses the draw has the same effect whatever conditions prevail on the day. In big fields especially, the draw can make an immense difference to results, even to the point where some horses badly drawn 'may just as well have stayed at home', as the saying goes in racing circles.

Despite all the evidence there are some punters who do not trouble themselves with this vital factor. This is folly. The result of the Temple Stakes run over five furlongs at Sandown in May, 2000 provides a good example. The going was heavy and it was known in advance that high numbers were likely to be favoured. However, in a field of only 10 runners, backers ignored the known effect of the draw and made Sampower Star, drawn on the outside at 3, favourite for the race.

The result was as follows:

		Draw
Winner:	Perryston View	10
Second:	Proud Native	8
Third:	Rambling Bear	9

| Fifth: | Sampower Star 11–8 fav | 3 |

beaten 5l, ¾l, 5l, 3l, a total of 13¾ lengths.

Enough said?

23
Criterion 16 – Breeding

Genetic influences in thoroughbred racehorses are very strong. One influence is that a stallion transmits its going preferences to its progeny. The tables below show this preference for the leading sires in so far as deviations from good ground are concerned. Where a sire appears in the No Preference box it may be assumed that the stallion and its progeny have no real preference and are equally at home on any ground.

FIRM – Marked Preference	
BATSHOOF	POLISH PRECEDENT
BE MY GUEST	PRIOLO
CAERLEON	PUISSANCE
CLANTIME	REPRIMAND
CLASSIC MUSIC	ROBELLINO
DAYJUR	ROCK CITY
DEPLOY	ROI DANZIG
EMARATI	SIBERIAN EXPRESS
GONE WEST	SILVER HAWK
GREEN DESERT	SOVIET STAR
GROOM DANCER	TAUFAN
IN THE WINGS	TIMELESS TIMES
KEEN	TIROL
MAZILIER	WAAJIB
MTOTO	WELDNAAS
PHARLY	WOODMAN

FIRM – SLIGHT PREFERENCE

ABSALOM	LAST TYCOON
ARAGON	MACHIAVELLIAN
BALLAD ROCK	MIDYAN
BELFORT	MOST WELCOME
CHILIBANG	NASHWAN
COZZENE	POLISH PATRIOT
DANCING BRAVE	RAINBOW QUEST
DANEHILL	ROYAL ACADEMY
DANZIG	SALSE
DARSHAAN	SALT DOME
DOWSING	SUPERLATIVE
ELA-MANA-MOU	TREASURE KAY
GENEROUS	WARNING
KAHYASI	

NO PREFERENCE

ANSHAN	MUJTAHID
BE MY CHIEF	MUSIC BOY
BE MY NATIVE	NIGHT SHIFT
BLUEBIRD	NINISKI
CADEAUX GENEREUX	NOMINATION
DANCING DISSIDENT	PENNINE WALK
DIESIS	PERSIAN HEIGHTS
DISTANT RELATIVE	PERUGINO
DISTINCTLY NORTH	PETONG
DIXIELAND BAND	PETORIUS
DOULAB	PIP'S PRIDE
FAYRUZ	PRINCE RUPERT
FORZANDO	RAMBO DANCER
GULCH	RED RANSOM
HIGHEST HONOUR	SHAADI
KALAGLOW	SHAREEF DANCER
KEFAAH	SHARROOD
KING OF SPAIN	SHERNAZAR
KNOWN FACT	STATOBLEST
KRIS	THEATRICAL
LEAR FAN	TINA'S PET
LOMOND	ZAFONIC
LYCIUS	

SOFT – Slight Preference

ALZAO	LAW SOCIETY
BAIRN	NEVER SO BOLD
BERING	NORDICO
BEVELED	OLD VIC
BROKEN HEARTED	PRIMO DOMINIE
COMMON GROUNDS	PRINCE SABO
CYRANO DE BERGERAC	RED SUNSET
DAMISTER	RIVERMAN
DIGAMIST	SADLER'S WELLS
FAIRY KING	SLIP ANCHOR
GLENSTAL	TRAGIC ROLE
INDIAN RIDGE	UNFUWAIN
KOMAITE	

SOFT – Marked Preference

CONTRACT LAW	PRESIDIUM
DON'T FORGET ME	RISK ME
DOYOUN	SCENIC
EFISIO	SHARPO
EL GRAN SENOR	SUPERPOWER
MARJU	ZILZAL
POLAR FALCON	

Therefore horses by the sires in the 'firm' tables will in all probability prefer firm and will usually, but not necessarily, dislike its opposite of soft. Progeny from the 'soft' tables may well dislike firm, but positively love soft, though here again the positive emphasised in the tables does not always imply a corresponding negative. Horses by sires with no preference, as we have already noted, will probably not have a preference one way or the other, or at least will be able to act reasonably well on any type of going. Alternatively, they may have a preference unique to themselves which cannot be inferred from the stallion.

It is possible that some newcomers to racing will not treat these stallion tables with the respect they undoubtedly deserve. 'Surely', the tyro might argue, 'something as particular as a liking for one kind of going or a dislike for another is so individual to each horse that its parentage has little to do with it'. In fact, though nothing of this sort is infallibly true in racing, a stallion's influence in that respect is one of the most solid rules in the entire sport for, by and large, a thoroughbred tends to take its physical characteristics from its sire. Faced with a horse unexposed on an extreme of going, you can be remarkably 'clued up' as to whether it will be able to produce its best form on it, while other punters are merely stumbling about in the dark.

National Hunt

There are those who assert that weight does not matter very much in National Hunt racing and that by contrast, jumping is the paramount factor in determining results, at least in steeplechases.

In my opinion such people are wrong about weight, and only partly correct about jumping. Two or three pounds might not make the difference they often do on the Flat, but 'over the sticks' it is still weight that is used to bring horses together in handicaps, and it is weight that separates them at the finish of a race.

That jumping is crucial in this branch of equine sport is surely self-evident. On the other hand it should be realised that speed and stamina are two other essential ingredients in the make-up of a successful National Hunt horse. An animal may be a very safe jumper, but it will not win races unless it is capable of laying up with and passing rivals at key moments while possessing the capacity to see out its races full of running at the business end of a contest.

What many people fail to understand is that jumping is just as important in hurdling as in chasing. Only a very superior hurdler jumps cleanly every time without touching the obstacles or losing momentum. Over a distance of two miles or more how a horse performs at the hurdles can make a difference of many lengths in determining where it finishes in a race.

Since form is a compound of weight, jumping ability, stamina, speed through a race and acceleration at the end of it, the problems presented by National Hunt racing are every bit as complex as those peculiar to the Flat. Few people really know how to go about solving this complexity from a betting point of view, and this section of the book, like the previous one for the Flat, takes one through every stage of analysing a lot of information that is relevant to the inherent problems. The object is to locate sound selections which can be backed with a reasonable expectation of overall success.

24
HANDICAPS

Form in handicaps can still be defined as recent past performance against the background of weight ratings and race grade but its assessment needs to be informed by a consideration of the special characteristics of jump racing. This will be dealt with in relation to race type from Criterion 17 onwards. As an introduction to these specific guidelines, however, we will once again examine the concept of 'instant handicapping' as applied to races over obstacles. Firstly something needs to be said about jumping form in general.

Races over jumps are now officially graded, as are Flat races, but there are some points of variation which reflect differences between the two branches of the sport.

This is the National Hunt scale:

> Class A Grade 1
> Class A Grade 2
> Class A Grade 3
> Class B
> Class C
> Class D
> Class E
> Class F
> Class G
> Class H

Thus, as on the Flat, there are 10 ranks. The difference between the top of the very top rank and the top of the bottom tier is again 4½ st, if seven pounds is unofficially allotted to each rank.

Over jumps, however, horses of the very highest class sometimes compete in handicaps, particularly in chases, whereas on the Flat such animals are expressly disqualified from doing so. On the Flat, therefore, all Group One, Group Two and Group Three events, and practically all Listed races, are non-handicaps. Under National Hunt rules, on the other hand, handicaps may extend as far up the scale as Grade 2 of Class A. Only Class A Grade 1 is an exclusively non-handicap grade in the manner of a Flat Group race. Also, at the other end of the scale, Class H is used to accommodate two special categories of National Hunt horse, namely hunter chasers and National Hunt Flat horses.

These few distinctions apart, the two scales are in essence much the same, and our basic form-reading methodology for the Flat can be applied equally well to National Hunt. A comparison of official weight rating related to grade of race for each horse, with the same data from every runner's most recent public run, is similarly valid as a measure of the most relevant form available and of the prospects that can be inferred from it.

25
INSTANT HANDICAPPING

Once again 100 races in a single, uninterrupted block, one for handicap chases and one for handicap hurdles, were used to provide some basic data from which to draw conclusions. Just as before, the sample is a fairly small one in relation to say, the total number of races in a season, but it will be adequate to confirm the author's experience of jump racing over many years in so far as handicap races over jumps are concerned.

The outcome of the survey of 100 steeplechases, arranged into a single 'handicap of results' was as follows:

SURVEY OF 100 HANDICAP CHASES

A 2-5 4-6 4-5 6-5 11-8 13-8 15-8 2-1 2-1 9-4 9-4 100-30 7-2 4-1 4-1 9-2 5-1 5-1 5-1 11-2 11-2 6-1 7-1 9-1

B 11-10 11-8 11-8 9-4 5-2 7-2 6-1 6-1 6-1 8-1

C 4-5 6-4 7-4 7-4 2-1 9-4 5-2 7-2 9-2 9-2 5-1 7-1 7-1

D 13-8 3-1 3-1 7-2 4-1 4-1 5-1 5-1 11-2 6-1 8-1 10-1 16-1

E 4-7 3-1 3-1 3-1 7-2 7-2 4-1 9-2 5-1 5-1 11-2 13-2 7-1 12-1 12-1

F 7-2 4-1 6-1 7-1 16-1 40-1

G 11-2 6-1 6-1 7-1 8-1

H 4-1 6-1 7-1

I 7-4

J 9-2 12-1

K 10-1 25-1

L 9-4 16-1 16-1 40-1

M

N 9-4

O

P

Q 12-1

The picture here is remarkably similar to the one derived from the survey of Flat handicaps. The same triangular pattern occurs to confirm that in handicap chases too horses near the top of the weights predominate among winners. As the handicap descends, winners get less and less to the point where they tail off to none at all (the biggest field in the survey was one of 18 runners).

Just as on the Flat, handicap chases were dominated by the five handicap positions A to E with 75 per cent of the total races in the survey won by them. There was some immediate falling off of the incidence of winners at F, then the strike rate fell dramatically.

Therefore in the instant handicapping method, the top five weights, including any horses set to carry equal fifth weight, should form the core of selections in handicap chases. Given the very impressive array of winners from the highest weighted horse of all, there is no need here for a special rule to deal with the most heavily burdened horses which was considered necessary for the Flat. Indeed, in this particular sample of handicap chases at least, a simple level-stakes bet on the top weight alone would have produced an outcome, including betting tax, close to the break-even point. It might be possible with just a little refinement to devise a system around top weights in handicap chases as a trouble-free automatic bet. One could certainly do a lot worse. If, however, the idea is to find the largest possible number of winners in these races, then it is necessary to go further down the handicap. Once the fifth position in the weights has been decided upon as the cut-off point there has to be some way of singling out the best bet or bets from the group of runners indicated thereby.

As with the Flat, once again the obvious way to narrow down the five favoured weights in a handicap chase is to consider probable starting prices. The price bands used for the Flat would not be helpful here, however, for the merest glance tells us that the odds about winners are on the whole much shorter. Therefore, a different set of odds groupings was adopted to reflect this change in the overall starting price picture.

The new price bands, together with the number of winners accruing in each, were as follows:

Up to 2–1	20 winners
9–4 to 4–1	28 winners
9–2 to 13–2	28 winners
7–1 to 10–1	13 winners
(including 7 winners at 7–1)	
11–1 or over	11 winners

Thus 56 per cent of all the winners started at from 9–4 to 13–2 inclusive. If this price range is extended to include the single price of 7–1 which alone accounted for seven winners in the survey, the percentage rises to a very impressive 63. Horses at 2–1 or less should be excluded because they do not represent value, given the comparatively low number of winners produced.

We now have a second simple rule with which to reinforce the basic strategy of considering only the top five weights in handicap chases: back only horses quoted at between 9–4 and 7–1 in the betting forecast of the newspaper consulted.

Once again the problem of the difference between actual starting prices and betting forecast estimates arises. Yet this is not really a significant drawback. The forecasts produced by representatives of the Press Association are in fact just as accurate in their own way at assessing the chance of runners based on form and expressed in prices, as is the racecourse market in producing odds which similarly reflect chances based on form *and* the opinion of backers expressed through the amount of money staked. The betting forecast can only be a substitute for the actual market in the Ring but it is still a very good substitute.

A more fundamental objection to our two-rule system for handicap chases is that fields in the sample were generally much smaller than those used for the Flat survey. It could be argued therefore that there is a statistical skew in the survey that tends to invalidate its conclusions. When a lot of races have fields of less than double figures, as is the case for handicap chases, the smaller number of runners outside the top five are bound to do much less well in percentage terms than when many races with much larger fields are considered. This is true, but there is still no getting away from the fact that 75 per cent of winners came from just five favoured weights. What was wanted was a straightforward and generally applicable overview which did not cloud the issue by placing artificial upper or lower limits on the size of fields.

So, a survey derived from taking the results of handicap chases just as they come is surely perfectly valid. The truth of the matter is that though many handicap chase fields are on the small side, the higher-weighted horses still visit the winner's enclosure more frequently than lighter-weighted rivals. Our system is doing no more than reflect the realities of the situation, imperfect as the survey in support of it may be in terms of strict statistical method.

Instant handicapping in steeplechases may indicate one, but very often more than one, runner in a race. In the latter case, as on the Flat, the final decision is left to the reader who may prefer to wait for single-selection races or make an informed choice from two or more qualifiers using other form precepts, or even back more than one horse in a race if the odds make this economic.

Thus no extra system rules are necessary. The Flat race rule of excluding apprentice jockeys is not suitable for jump racing – in National Hunt sport there are many competent riders who are not fully fledged professional jockeys but who, by and large, do an excellent job on their mounts. Two rules alone, operated in handicap chases, where small fields are the norm, may produce many winners at sound though not spectacular starting prices.

When we turn to consider handicap hurdles, the situation is different and far less encouraging for the backer. The results of the survey of 100 races of this type revealed that the reputation of handicap hurdles for being especially difficult is perfectly justified.

SURVEY OF 100 HANDICAP HURDLES

A   1-3 7-4 2-1 5-2 100-30 4-1 6-1 11-1

B   4-6 5-4 15-8 2-1 2-1 2-1 4-1 9-2 6-1 6-1 9-1 12-1 12-1 14-1 25-1

C   8-11 11-8 13-8 7-4 2-1 5-2 3-1 4-1 5-1 6-1 13-2 13-2

D   5-4 5-2 3-1 7-2 9-2 5-1 8-1 10-1 20-1

E   2-1 4-1 6-1 13-2 13-2 8-1 8-1 8-1 10-1 12-1 18-1

F   10-11 evens 9-4 11-4 100-30 9-2 6-1 6-1 10-1 10-1 10-1

G   7-4 7-2 7-2 11-2 11-2 6-1 6-1 7-1 8-1 66-1

H   4-1 11-2 7-1 7-1 12-1 12-1 20-1

I   5-4 4-1 11-2 8-1 9-1 14-1

J   6-1 14-1 25-1

K   9-4 7-1

L   4-6 12-1

M   7-2 12-1

N   6-1 20-1

The largest field in the survey had 22 runners. With no winners below 14th position, clearly low weights in these races must be avoided even more scrupulously than in other handicaps.

The overall picture is again triangular, but this time the shape is neither so clear nor so defined as in earlier surveys, with the triangle itself dominated by a rectangle within it emanating from B to F. The consequence of this blurring is that the handicap snapshot here is of less value when trying to discover an 'edge' that can be exploited against the bookmaker.

Winners in depth are found in consecutive positions as far down the weights as the eighth or even ninth position, whilst the highest weights of all cannot be said to be decisively favoured over those slightly further down. In fact the optimum range for winners is B to G, that is the six positions immediately below the top weight. Positions B to G accounted for no less than 68 per cent of winners.

Keeping to just five positions as a possible system focus in the style of previous versions of instant handicapping would yield 58 per cent winners, when the best five consecutive positions, B to F, are taken. But would one be justified in singling out this group as the sole material for betting when A and G, and even H and I, are so close to its component positions in terms of winners? Betting on B–F alone would exclude A, G, H and I, all good sources of winners. The alternative of a group including these positions would be so large that perhaps four, five or more qualifiers might be left after other, not too stringent, criteria have been applied to weed out the weakest runners.

Lacking an outstanding, small grouping therefore, probably the wisest thing to do is to abandon the basic instant handicapping concept as a hard-and-fast system rule. All that can really be inferred of value from the survey is the fact that when for some other sound reason a horse is backed in the B to G section of the handicap, it is well over 2–1 on (32–68) that it will be in the winning area of the handicap. Some readers might find this reassuring.

An analysis of the starting prices of winners in the races surveyed is similarly unhelpful. The findings are summarised in tabular form – with each X signifying a win – in order to make the point as graphically as possible, although the same price bands as for handicap chases have been used.

Up to 2–1	XXXXXXXXXXXXXXXXXXXXX
9–4 to 4–1	XXXXXXXXXXXXXXXXXXX
9–2 to 13–2	XXXXXXXXXXXXXXXXXXXXXXXX
7–1 to 10–1	XXXXXXXXXXXXXXXX
11–1 or over	XXXXXXXXXXXXXXXXX

The even distribution of winners across the full range of prices means that here too no statistical bias exists for the punter to exploit. Also the 21 horses which won at 2–1 or less suggests that when form horses do win one of these races, the odds available for them are likely to represent very poor value.

In handicap hurdles therefore, the instant handicapping concept is not really a viable one. Neither weight nor price can be used to pinpoint winners and to the best of my knowledge nor can any other statistical criterion.

The reason for this is not hard to fathom. There are a great many moderate horses that can be trained with some prospect of winning a handicap hurdle of some kind. Provided it has just enough speed and stamina to keep in touch in lowly company and has been properly schooled with the necessary racecourse experience, a very indifferent performer may be able to take advantage of a handicapping system that gives every runner the chance of its moment of glory. Even so, some horses are beyond redemption but, with the exception of novice hurdles, in no other sort of race do so many poor horses regularly compete to the extent that they do in handicap hurdles. No wonder that in the Racecourse Guide at the back of this book handicap hurdles feature in our 'worst races for favourites' slot more often than any other category of race.

The conclusion is inescapable. Strictly speaking one should refrain from betting in handicap hurdles for the simple reason that there are, as a general rule, no more difficult races for the backer in the whole of racing. However, the punter attending a race meeting might want an interest in every race, or one could see handicap hurdles as a source of the occasional winning outsider needed for betting plans. To cover this situation, Criterion 18 is included, which offers a theory for finding winners for these races. First, however, we will set out some specific guidelines for handicap chases.

26
CRITERION 17 – HANDICAP CHASES

Instant handicapping showed how the vital factors of weight and price can be converted into a simple formula for races of this kind. Even if you do not use the weights and betting forecast in the way suggested, they must still be weighed carefully in the balance of form for the conventional analysis of handicap chases. Jumping is the other factor that needs to be assessed in such an analysis.

This is really a job for the expert race reader and one, moreover, who is able to see a great deal of the racing over fences which takes place during the season. This in effect means someone professionally engaged in racing, although not even a professional can view every race on every course. However, there are several ways in which jumping can be assessed from the armchair, perhaps not as effectively as the ideal, but for all that, reasonably accurately.

1 Post-race comments in the official form book can be most instructive. Every runner's performance is covered by such comments, and a horse which jumped cleanly throughout a race will have no tell-tale comments about blundering at its fences.

2 The form book sometimes gives very specific clues. For instance 'j.w.' is a comment that is used occasionally. It means in fact that a horse which 'jumped well' put in an outstanding round. The sparing use of this deliberate understatement makes it a comment that should be especially noted when assessing a chaser's prospects in near-at-hand engagements.

3 Another way of assessing the jumping talents of any horse is to look at its performances and, where applicable, its last-time-out performance in particular, judged against the background of the courses recognised as being difficult in a jumping sense.

A horse which ran well to win or finish close up at a meeting where the fences are noted as 'testing', 'stiff' or 'severe' in our Racecourse Guide has undoubtedly put up a good performance. Even if a horse got tired and struggled at one or more of the closing fences as the pace of its race gradually built up towards the finish, a good run on a severe track is worth far more in form terms than a similar run on an easy course.

4   A final indicator of jumping ability depends on a straight-forward interpretation of the six-figure form lines which appear on racecards. A chaser which has fallen, unseated rider, refused or pulled up in several of its most recent races is obviously a suspect jumper, or at least one running out of its class. Such a horse is likely to sacrifice its chance at the fences, and there must be a serious doubt as to whether it will complete the course in a current engagement. Only a significant drop in grade might enable it to compete on equal jumping terms with lesser rivals than it has been meeting.

Picking the winners of handicap chases need not be too daunting a task therefore. One's choice should be based on the following criteria:

a) weight indicates that it is one of the better class horses in the race;
b) recent runs, and preferably the most recent of all, have indicated a sound level of current form and jumping ability;
c) a quote among the first three or four in the betting.

A horse that meets these requirements could provide a ready-made winner, or at least one that, on form, certainly ought to be.

27
CRITERION 18 – HANDICAP HURDLES

Here are a few hints to help those who insist on betting in these races:

1 If a horse is to win a hurdle race against seasoned animals of roughly equal ability, it will need experience and plenty of it. Very few hurdlers, whatever their natural talent, realise their potential without this prerequisite. The surest way to establish whether a horse has such experience is to check whether it has already won a handicap hurdle race. Regardless of the grade of the race and irrespective of how it performed last time out, no bet should be laid on a handicap hurdler which has only won, so far, in novice company.

2 We have seen that there is a definite statistically favoured weight range in handicap hurdles beginning somewhere just below top weight. This means that horses near the bottom of the weights in these races are not likely to win because they are usually outclassed by better hurdlers.

3 Some horses are able to run up a sequence of wins in handicap hurdles. The reason is that extra weight does not easily stop a horse with a measure of hurdling talent at the top of its form. Any winner of a handicap hurdle may survive a quite steep rise in its official rating and still win again, if not immediately, then at least in the not-too-distant future.

4 By contrast, weight tells in hurdle races over the longer distances, particularly when the ground is soft or heavy. Therefore, one's betting response to weight and weight rises should be modified in races of 2m 6f or more.

5 In races over shorter distances up to 2m 2f (2½ miles is the 'in-between distance) the ability to quicken at the end of a hurdle race is important, far more important than in chasing. Any evidence of such speed in a horse's racing record is a big plus

which, when combined with good or improving form last time out, suggests a horse which has what it takes to win.

6	Keep stakes to a minimum if betting in handicap hurdles however good a horse's chance seems to be. Appearances can be deceptive in races of this kind.

28
NON-HANDICAPS

As we have seen, there are a number of important differences between National Hunt and Flat racing, but there is also much that is common to both sports. In the general matter of reading form and the betting-forecast odds derived from it, we are justified in repeating the statistically based prescriptions for staking on non-handicaps according to price which could be applied on the Flat. National Hunt favourites on the whole have a slightly better record, but the difference is not all that great. The prices of favourites laid down to determine specific courses of betting action on the Flat are identical over jumps:

1   If a horse is quoted at odds-on, there is a greater chance of it winning than losing. You should not oppose it.

2   Favourites quoted at between evens and 6–4 are more likely to win than lose.

3   Those put in as favourite at from 13–8 to 11–4 inclusive will win and lose in the approximate proportions of one winner to every three losers. There may be occasions when such favourites are worth backing.

4   There is only about a 10 per cent chance that a favourite quoted at 3–1 or more in the betting forecast will win.

For the person who is comfortable with the principle of automatic rules in betting, the four precepts set out above may prove invaluable. Even those who are not prepared to be quite so restricted in how they bet would almost certainly benefit from keeping them in mind as general standards in non-handicap betting. It is possible to be more open-minded however, depending especially on the category of race in which you are considering having a bet.

29
CRITERION 19 – NOVICE HURDLES

Novice hurdle races are open to horses which, before the beginning of the season, have not won a hurdle race of any kind. Here are some tips for dealing with them.

1 The technique for jumping hurdles is different to that for steeplechasing. It is flatter and faster, and some horses have it naturally. Others must learn it.

   Either way, as we have noted already in the case of handicap hurdlers, all horses need experience over hurdles before they can shine, even in lowly company. Schooling at home is no substitute for the racecourse. Some horses need a whole season in novice company before they master the technique tolerably well; they will almost certainly never aspire to be more than average in the hurdling sphere.

2 For the same reasons one should generally avoid Flat horses having their first run over hurdles. Similarly horses coming on from National Hunt Flat races, even if they have won a 'bumper', should be given time to prove themselves in the new arena. The relatively few horses from these two categories which win first time up are more than made up for by the army of horses that do not.

3 Also, again because of the demands imposed by the obstacles, hurdlers seldom win if backward. A racecourse run to bring a hurdler to its peak is far more necessary than for a Flat racer or a chaser.

   A good ploy is to regularly check the form book for those novice hurdlers noted as 'backward' or a 'bit backward' on their initial outing. They will definitely improve next time out.

4 The introduction of penalties for winners in novice races has reduced quite noticeably the number of hurdlers which run up a sequence of victories, contrary to what happens in handicap hurdles where experienced horses seem to be able to defy weight

increases. Certainly there has been a decline in the strike rate of first and second favourites in novice hurdles which is difficult to account for otherwise.

5 A win last time out, therefore, is not always the recommendation it ought to be. With prices on the cramped side, it may be better to look instead for improving sorts which ran a good second or third last time.

30
CRITERION 20 – NOVICE CHASES

Novice chases are mostly about jumping not speed. They have the reputation of being one of racing's biggest lotteries because it is believed that 'dodgy' jumpers abound in them. As a consequence betting in novice chases, even on favourites, is almost universally considered a high-risk business.

Yet again, this category of race need not be excluded from the betting repertoire provided one learns to recognise the types of horse involved. Timing is also very important.

There are three main sorts of novice chaser:

1   One significant category, though a minority, consists of the type of animal which has always been seen by connections as a good chasing prospect. Such expectations will have been based on breeding, physical conformation and the general demeanour of the horse. Any runs over hurdles, which will almost certainly have been limited in number, have been primarily for experience as part of a horse's education. Some top-class chasing sorts bypass hurdles altogether.

   Such horses can be difficult to identify for those not intimately connected with the sport. The stay-at-home enthusiast must rely on racing annuals and the daily racing press to gain information about the most prominent among them. But those that do not attract publicity can be extremely difficult to spot.

   They will generally be racing over fences for the first time as five-, six- or even seven-year-olds. Their hurdling career, if they had one at all, will have been short and unambitious. They will not be rushed however, and will probably have one or two runs in lowly novice chase company before suddenly being catapulted into a much higher grade. This is a decisive point in their career, the stage at which to step in and bet, provided that a genuine, top-class chasing prospect has been correctly identified. A win in top novice company may be the prelude to a sequence of victories, but prices thereafter will be on the short side.

2   A second category of novice chaser is the good hurdler which is sent chasing as it grows older and at the point in time where it has begun to lose its speed in races over the smaller obstacles. Many horses of this type make the grade over fences and some of them go on to take their place in the very top rank of chasers. Complete failures over fences are comparatively few.

   Though courage is needed on the part of the backer, the time to bet on animals like these is on their steeplechase debuts. If they are successful, prices are bound to be short in subsequent runs and a victory is much less assured when they take on the better class of chaser at the next stage in their career.

3   Finally there are horses which failed in the main as hurdlers and are sent chasing if not exactly as a last resort, then at least because it has become obvious that they lack the ability to compete with speedier animals in the hurdling arena.

   Very few of these horses do well over fences and should be studiously avoided by the shrewd student of form. There will be exceptions, but their success is unpredictable. It is much safer to disregard such types altogether, at least until they have proved themselves by a win in fair company.

In the lower grades, novice chasers in general, once they have had a bit of racing, are sometimes a sound bet in handicaps against more experienced chasers. They get into handicap chases with a low weight and can jump round well clear of jaded horses with a lot of races under the saddle.

   This does not apply to the better class of handicap steeplechaser however, where jumping ability, in most cases born of experience, is paramount. There has always been a tendency, among some trainers at least, to run an exceptional novice against good, seasoned chasers too soon. The wisdom of trying to strike while the iron is hot may be justified from the connections' point of view but, as far as betting is concerned, it is a sound dictum never to back a novice in top chasing company. The stiffer the task for the novice, the more this applies. The history book is full of inglorious failures, and the few exceptions are there to prove the rule.

31
CRITERION 21 – CONDITIONS RACES

Never bet in National Hunt Flat races because form is so unexposed. However, non-handicaps for experienced hurdlers and chasers meeting on more-or-less equal terms tend to be won by form horses at any grade. The form figures cited in Criterion 4, as well as the general prescriptions based on betting forecast prices set out in the opening part of this section on jump non-handicaps, may assist readers to find plenty of winners.

32
CRITERION 22 – HUNTER CHASES

Fewer favourites win than once was the case, but the better class animals keep winning and are capable of running up a sequence. They should be followed until beaten.

By and large a young hunter with good point-to-point form is a better proposition than the National Hunt 'has-beens' which sometimes end their careers in this sphere of competition. Readers are referred to the BLUEPRINT method in Part 2, one element of which consists of a method for hunter chasers.

33
CRITERION 23 – DISTANCE, GOING AND FITNESS

As a general rule and excluding the top yards, the legion of jump trainers and permit holders up and down the country are far less focused than the Flat training fraternity when it comes to placing their horses. Over jumps horses are often run at the wrong distance or on the wrong type of course or on the wrong going. The really gifted student of form can sometimes cash in.

Over fences, two-and-a-half miles is a specialist distance. Especially on good going on an easy to only moderately testing track, the distance specialist will beat genuine two- or three-milers nearly every time when it has its trip.

Over hurdles the difference between two miles and two-and-a-half miles, or between two-and-a-half miles and three miles, is not nearly so important.

Apart from the summer and autumn months when only horses needing a fast surface race under National Hunt rules, most jumpers are at their best on good ground, although they can handle soft. However, very heavy ground will obviously inconvenience some winter jumpers, though others have a particular liking for 'bottomless' going. In this respect it should be remembered that official going of 'heavy' over jumps is very different to the much less severe 'heavy' of the Flat.

It might be thought that because they compete over longer distances and often in tougher conditions than Flat animals, National Hunt horses would need a longer period of recuperation between races. However, the statistics quoted in this connection on pages 126–7 of this book suggest, paradoxically perhaps, that the most successful jumpers are those running within a relatively short time of their last outing. The figures here are very similar under both codes of racing, and jumpers, like the Flat horses, do best in statistical terms when reappearing within a fortnight.

34
CRITERION 24 – BREEDING

Breeding as it affects performance, though evidently significant in imparting class and ability, is much less useful over jumps compared with the Flat to the form student who looks for a liking for an extreme of going.

Some stallions, however, impart a strong preference for heavy ground to their sons and daughters racing over hurdles and fences. Such stallions are listed in the right-hand column of the table below. The progeny of sires on the left-hand side are in the main equally at home on all reasonable types of going.

Any Going	Soft/Heavy
ABSALOM	ARDROSS
BUCKSKIN	BERING
CAERLEON	CARLINGFORD CASTLE
CALLERNISH	CRASH COURSE
CELTIC CONE	CYBORGO
ELA-MANA-MOU	DEEP RUN
FURRY GLEN	DOMINION
IDIOT'S DELIGHT	GLINT OF GOLD
KAMBALDA	KING'S RIDE
LE BAVARD	NEARLY A HAND
LE MOSS	NORDANCE
MANDALUS	OVER THE RIVER
NICHOLAS BILL	RELKINO
NORWICH	ROLFE
OATS	ROSELIER
ORCHESTRA	SADLER'S WELLS
PHARDANTE	STRONG GALE
SULA BULA	THE PARSON
	TORUS

35
Five Golden Rules of Handicap Betting (Flat or Jumps)

1 With the exception of instant handicapping based on a statistical approach, all the form-related methods of picking winners in the preceding sections are, in the main, more effective in higher rather than the lower grades of handicap.

2 Keep the bulk of handicap betting to fields with a maximum of about 10 runners, and never bet in a field of more than about 16 runners if trying to find the winner in a single pick.

 Simple mathematics dictate that the fewer runners opposing the selection, the greater the chance of being on the winner in those races where every horse has a theoretically equal chance on an official estimate of form.

3 As a general strategy back more than one horse in the race when betting in handicaps. Two single points on two horses is better value than one point each-way on a single selection, unless there is a very good reason to know that the latter has a quite exceptional chance of reaching a place at remunerative odds.

4 When a horse is priced at 10–1 or over in the actual betting market on a handicap race, bet at Tote odds if available.

5 Do not bet more than one can comfortably afford to lose and never chase your losses.

36
FIVE GOLDEN RULES OF BETTING IN NON-HANDICAPS
(FLAT OR JUMPS)

1 In a non-handicap race the favourite almost always has the best theoretical chance of winning. There needs to be a good reason for opposing it with a bet on another runner.

2 Do not bet beyond the first three in the betting except when there is statistical evidence to suggest that a broader approach may be successful.

3 Good form last time out is the primary qualification for a potential winner. This is even more important in a non-handicap than a handicap.

4 Non-handicaps for older horses are dominated by a small group of elite trainers. The overall and current form of a top stable is usually as significant as the actual form of individual horses. This applies particularly to maiden races.

    Two-year-old stakes races, however, are much more competitive and are won by trainers at all levels in the training hierarchy.

5 Do not bet more than one can comfortably afford to lose and never chase losses.

37
THE RULES OF STAKING

There is absolutely nothing wrong with level stakes as a staking system, though in practice it requires a lot of discipline always to have the same amount on every single selection. Most backers vary their stakes according to fancy and a personal estimate of the strength of a selection. This is the opposite principle to level stakes. For most people, not blessed with unerring judgement, it is one of the worst ways to stake, despite its popularity. Big stakes tend to go on losers, small stakes on to winners – not always but often enough to make this a losing game in which the backer does not exploit successes to the full financially.

The problem with level stakes as a method, strictly applied, is that the accumulation of a worthwhile profit is inevitably slow, so that the patience of Job is required on the backer's part. One way out of this bind is, very gradually, to increase or decrease the general level of staking as profits build up or losses mount. A lot of money-management skill is needed for this strategy, but the effort is well worth making.

VALUE

Where bets are not placed at starting price, the backer should seek 'value' in the odds taken about horses backed. However, if anyone could devise a method of accurately assessing value in the odds in relation to a horse's precise mathematical and form chance, this would in effect be the infallible racing system. All the backer would have to do would be to bet only when the odds on offer were above the selection's true chance of winning, which could similarly be expressed in odds. In the end a credit balance would be bound to accrue.

In terms of reality, however, one way in which the punter can improve his position against the bookmakers' trading edge is to keep to small fields. Fewer runners against a selection improves its chance of winning in mathematical terms. Also, the bookmakers' over-round, which is explained in Chapter 52, is less in small fields.

VARIATION IN THE ODDS

The use of a staking plan, even when the backer is in the unlikely position of always being able to take an exact price, can never be a perfect solution to betting. This is because it is impossible to predict in advance the pattern of winners and losers which, if known, would enable punters to maximise profits. They would simply back the winners and disregard the losers!

For most backers who must bet some of the time away from the course or the betting shop where definite odds are obtainable, the lesser difficulty of variation between betting forecast quotations and the eventual starting price can be enough to reduce the efficiency of automatically regulated staking. However ingeniously devised a plan is in relation to the type of selection, the probable percentage of winners and the expected level of odds, frequent deviations from the expected starting price norm will upset the long-term financial balance of a great many staking methods. This will reduce the chances of obtaining maximum gain or minimum loss from any series of wagers.

INCREASING STAKES AFTER LOSERS

Staking plans of this type should generally be avoided. By definition they involve chasing losses and, in the real world of a limited betting bank, winners may not pay for losers as they are expected to do. Too often increasing stakes on a losing run gets backers into deep trouble quickly and, whatever the theory, in practice they find themselves forced to give up with only a hefty loss to show for their endeavours.

INCREASING STAKES AFTER WINNERS

Such systems can do little harm and may do some good if used sensibly. By increasing stakes gradually, using cash from the bookmaker, it may be possible to enhance profits significantly. However, the strategy is as much dependent on the pattern of winners and losers as any other form of staking plan. An adverse pattern can occur for any staking plan, even one calling for increasing stakes after winners. One objection to all plans of this type is that it is virtually impossible to avoid having the largest stake of all on the loser which terminates a run of winners.

Increasing stakes after winners works best with selections that give a high percentage of winners, and that means favourites or near-favourites for the most part.

Staking 1/10, 1/12 or 1/15 of the betting bank and then increasing or decreasing the stake by the same fraction throughout according to the ebb and flow of winners and losers is a fundamentally sound method of betting although, without an exceptionally high percentage of winners, the conversion of wins into a worthwhile, overall profit can be a lengthy process.

MULTIPLE BETS

Bets of the Yankee, Heinz, Lucky Fifteen or Round-the-Clock variety should be avoided by the serious backer. Unless nearly all selections are correct, the high wastage in stakes from losers can eat into profits in a devastating way in bets involving full cover on doubles, trebles and accumulators on a larger number of selections. These bets are promoted by bookmaking firms in their advertising and with good reason from their point of view. Singles are the key to the layers' safe.

The 'WEEKENDER' bet, however, which is the final system in Part 2 of this book, is a sound example of a multiple bet. This is because it works on the principle of permutation and not of full cover. Full cover immediately writes off a disproportionately high number of individual bets within the whole, every time a loser is backed. Limited permutation, on the other hand, budgets for losers and can enhance profits by exploiting winners to the full at reduced stakes in the form of fewer bets when compared with the unrealistic blanket coverage of a Yankee or Heinz.

GROUP BETTING

A generation ago one national newspaper's leading tipsters always gave three selections for every handicap in their panel of tips for a meeting. In a more demanding age this concept of finding 'the winner in three' has been quietly consigned to history, but from a staking point of view in handicaps it remains a very sound approach.

As already stated in one of our 'Golden Rules', several selections to win a handicap outright is superior mathematically to the drastically reduced odds for a place that are part of each-way bets. Backing a small group to win against the field – two, three or even more if prices allow it – is the recommended basic procedure for all handicaps. Even the biggest handicaps such as the Royal Hunt Cup, the Stewards' Cup and the Cambridgeshire, can be tackled in this way with real prospects of success. The full methodology for this form of group betting is described in Part 3.

If one embraces the concept of several against the field, individual wins may be smaller but much more frequent. In the long run one should gain financially by adopting this more cautious approach.

RACECOURSE BETTING

Many people who go racing for an afternoon's sport are often in the position of backing a couple of winners, but somehow contrive to emerge with a loss on the day. They may even have an exceptional day and back more winners than that but still have very little to show financially for their efforts. Faulty staking is nearly always the cause. Add to this all the days when the typical racegoer does not find a winner at all and the result is that, combined with the high entrance money and other expenses, visits to the racecourse can be a very expensive business indeed.

Following the rules set out below, however, will give one a sporting chance of getting it right on the racecourse, unlike so many fellow racing enthusiasts.

RACECOURSE STAKING PLAN

1 Stake 1 point on a single selection in non-handicaps (including any claiming race not labelled a 'handicap'), until a change of stake is called for by these rules.

2 In handicaps stake ½ point and ½ point on two horses, or ⅓ point on each of three horses, until a change of stake is called for.

3 If a winner is backed at evens or odds against (or money is at least doubled on total outlay in a handicap), stakes should be increased by 1 point in subsequent races (plus ½ point twice or plus ⅓ point three times in handicaps).

4 If an odds-on winner is backed (or winnings do not double the total outlay in a handicap), stakes should not be changed as a result of that winner, except when Rule 7 applies.

5 A single-selection winner at odds-on (or a winner which does not at least double the total money staked in a handicap) does not count as a 'winning race' for system purposes, except in Rule 7.

6 If a second winner is backed at evens or odds against (or the total money staked is at least doubled in a handicap, making a second winning race), stakes should be increased by 1 point (plus ½ point twice or plus ⅓ point three times in a handicap) on the NEXT RACE ONLY. If a loser, the stake reverts to 2 points or the handicap equivalent on several horses.

7 After three winners at the meeting, whether at odds-on or odds against (including any handicap winners where the stake was not at least doubled), stakes must be IMMEDIATELY reduced on all remaining races to ½ point and must not be increased again under any circumstances.
   Stakes on handicaps are thereby reduced to ¼ point for each of two horses, or ⅙ point for each of three horses.

All this looks horribly complicated at first sight, but it is really quite simple. After one winning race at evens or better the stakes are increased to 2 points, and after two winning races the stakes rises to the maximum of 3 points before reverting to 2 points or even only ½ point if three winners at any price have been found.

One variation of this racecourse staking system is allowed, although some readers may look askance, having been lectured in the section on level stakes about the inadvisability of varying staking according to personal whim. This second version permits the backer to choose between the next race only *or* the next-but-one race only, when increasing to 3 points after a second 100 per cent-plus winning race. It may or may not have anything to do with the non-mathematical 'law of averages', but winner-loser-winner, which Americans call the 'skip-hit' technique in betting, is often a more achievable sequence than two consecutive winners. Be that as it may, provided there are at least two races left on the card in which to bet, the exceptionally skilled punter could well benefit from the element of selectivity implied in taking such an approach. With or without the corollary however, this racecourse staking plan is founded on a betting strategy that is eminently sensible.

One view put forward by gamblers of the less cautious kind is that one should always play up winnings when ahead, thus going for a really big profit. This is fair enough up to a point, but not to the extent that all the gains so far accrued are put at serious risk.

The rules of the recommended system are common sense and represent a compromise between trying to maximise profits in a sensible way and 'going for broke'. The plan is based on what might be called the principle of 'reasonable maximum expectation'. Winnings are played up from early successes in the hope of making a worthwhile profit on the day, but not at the risk of handing all gains made back to the bookmakers. If three winners have been found on a visit to the racecourse, one has become a hostage to fortune. Therefore stakes near the end of the card are reduced, not continually increased, the opposite of the approach that would be adopted by the out-and-out gambler.

This plan is worth a try when next visiting the racecourse. It may be better, however, to test it out on some cards from a newspaper before actually visiting the course in order to find out if it is suitable. One should soon see the point of a plan which aims to strike a balance between the actual, the probable and the only remotely possible.

Here is an example of the plan in action:

		Basic stake	Adjusted stake (if any)	Result	Profit/ loss
1st race	Non-handicap	1 pt	—	Lost	−1
2nd race	Handicap	½ pt ½ pt	—	Winner 4–1	+1½
3rd race	Handicap	½ pt ½ pt	½ pt ½ pt	Lost	−2
4th race	Non-handicap	1 pt	1 pt	Won 7–1	+14
5th race	Handicap	½ pt ½ pt	1 pt 1 pt	Lost	−3
6th race	Non-handicap	1 pt	1 pt	Won 4–6	+1⅓
7th race	Handicap	—	¼ pt ¼ pt	Lost	−½
				Total:	+10⅓

Level stakes: −1, +1½, −1, +7, −1, +⅔, −1. Total: +5⅙

This plan will usually improve the level-stakes position given some winners, but it is only fair to show also how things can go wrong if there is an unfavourable pattern of results.

Below can be seen what happens if the three winners at 4–6, 4–1 and 7–1 are rearranged in the very worst possible order:

		Basic stake	**Adjusted stake (if any)**	**Result**	**Profit/ loss**
1st race	Non-handicap	1 pt	—	Won 7–1	+7
2nd race	Handicap	½ pt ½ pt	½ pt ½ pt	Winner 4–1	+3
3rd race	Handicap	½ pt ½ pt	1 pt 1 pt	Lost	–3
4th race	Non-handicap	1 pt	1 pt	Lost	–2
5th race	Handicap	½ pt ½ pt	½ pt ½ pt	Lost	–2
6th race	Non-handicap	1 pt	1 pt	Won 4–6	+1⅓
7th race	Handicap	—	¼ pt ¼ pt	Lost	–½
					Total: +3⅚

Thus even when the winners are put in the worst possible order, the level-stakes situation is only 1⅓ points better, which is a very creditable performance for the staking plan.

It seems only fair to change things round one final time with a view to putting the plan in the best possible light:

		Basic stake	**Adjusted stake (if any)**	**Result**	**Profit/ loss**
1st race	Non-handicap	1 pt	—	Won 4–6	+⅔
2nd race	Handicap	½ pt ½ pt	—	Lost	–1
3rd race	Handicap	½ pt ½ pt	—	Winner 4–1	+1½
4th race	Non-handicap	1 pt	1 pt	Won 7–1	+14
5th race	Handicap	—	¼ pt ¼ pt	Lost	–½
6th race	Non-handicap	—	¼ pt ¼ pt	Lost	–½
7th race	Handicap	—	¼ pt ¼ pt	Lost	–½
					Total: +13⅔

This is quite significantly superior to level stakes. Hence the recommendation for the plan. Without being overly ambitious, thereby risking a serious dissipation of any gain, there is a real prospect of boosting profits and making a day at the races worthwhile in financial terms.

It always pays, however, when contemplating the use of any staking plan to work out the worst-case scenario and what that will mean in terms of total financial liability. In this case that liability is not 7 points at level stakes. It is worse than that and comes about only if one winner is backed and this winner occurs in the worst possible position in the progression. On any seven-race card this is what could happen:

1st race	Won evens	+1
2nd race	Lost	−2
3rd race	Lost	−2
4th race	Lost	−2
5th race	Lost	−2
6th race	Lost	−2
7th race	Lost	−2
	Total:	−11

A single winner at odds-on would not be a problem because the expensive stake increase is only triggered by a winner at odds against, or as in this case, by one at evens. The above sequence may seem unlikely, but it is by no means a freak result. It is shown here in fairness to the reader who has the right to be fully informed about any bet which these pages might inspire. That said, I believe the racecourse plan is still a good one and well worth a trial for anyone who is prepared to accept a little extra risk for the possibility, and in my view the probability, of quite a bit more gain.

STAKING LEVELS

The Golden Rule of all betting will stand repeating yet again – never bet more than you can afford to lose, and never chase your losses.

38
BETTING ON HORSES – FORM, THE VITAL KEY

From time to time the Government of the day appoints a Royal Commission charged with looking into various aspects of the gambling industry. In 1978 one such Commission did something none of its predecessors had done before and which its successors have not attempted since. It enquired into the relationship between punters and bookmakers, specifically with a view to establishing whether the former has any realistic chance of winning at the expense of the latter.

The studies the Commission had carried out went into considerable detail and were quite complicated from a statistical point of view but, broadly speaking, it came to the conclusion that horses at short prices were much better material for the punter than outsiders.

Over the quarter of a century before the 1978 Commission this situation had remained remarkably constant, even if things varied somewhat from year to year. It was found that if all horses which started at 6–4 on, or shorter, could somehow have been backed by one punter, that punter would actually have shown a small amount of profit on the total outlay. The fact that every horse in this odds range was considered means that the random principle alone was tested. No attempt was made to pick and choose by the application of form criteria of any kind. What would have been the result, therefore, had the imaginary punter been able to bring to the problem the kind of winner-finding aids discussed in the present book cannot be known, but if form has any value at all in racing, then the outcome must surely have been even more advantageous.

The Royal Commission also found that, in the long period covered by its survey, backing every horse priced at over 9–1 and less than 20–1 would have resulted in losses amounting to something in the region of 35 per cent of turnover. With horses at 20–1 or more the picture was even bleaker for the punter – a loss of about 70 per cent of total stakes would have accumulated over the years.

The 1978 Commission's findings were not new, however, and nor was the type of investigation it had conducted original. Its work had been largely anticipated by E. Lenox Figgis who in the world of gambling was better known by his pseudonym of 'Midas'. Figgis, a chartered accountant and actuary by profession, pursued his interest in probability and gambling to the point where he published under his own name *Focus on Gambling* in 1951. This book was issued by the firm of Arthur Barker Ltd and in it Figgis considered all the most popular gambles of the day. Football pools, greyhounds, cards and horse racing were among them, with much of his most interesting material being presented in a brilliant series of appendices.

In Appendix XVII Figgis surveyed the complete starting price returns for the 1951 Flat racing season. He found that backing all horses which started at 4–1 on or shorter showed a profit on outlay of almost 10 per cent. Horses with a probability of winning of between approximately 30 per cent and 20 per cent according to the starting price (odds of 5–2 to 4–1) accumulated an overall loss of around 4 per cent on turnover. Longshots priced at 20–1 or more produced a loss of 77 per cent. Throughout his survey Figgis adhered to the random principle of betting by which every horse at a given price or in a given price range was included in the reckoning.

The analysis of E. Lenox Figgis, confirmed by the Royal Commission nearly 30 years later, was replicated in one way or another in the years that followed by a series of studies, mostly American, undertaken by professional economists, academic statisticians and games theorists, as well as by several authorities on gambling. The exact rates of loss for various odds and price ranges differs at various times and in various circumstances, but the broad conclusion has always been the same. Short-priced horses in the odds-on category, which can sometimes be extended to include those at a shade of odds against, will often randomly produce a profit, although nowadays in Britain not nearly enough profit to offset betting tax at the current off-course rate of 9 per cent. As the odds lengthen, the more the backer can expect to lose in percentage terms, with rank outsiders a complete disaster from a random point of view, a clear warning to those punters habituated to backing them.

Anyone who came to this manual therefore with the preconceived opinion that betting is a 'mug's game', that 'there is only one winner – the bookmaker', and so on, must surely revise their views to some extent. Betting on horses, even random betting, can sometimes pay.

However, the imprimatur bestowed by the Royal Commission obviously requires modification from the point of view of the practical needs and desires of the ordinary backer. The gains accruing from very short-priced horses were tiny in comparison with the outlay that would have been involved in achieving them. It is very difficult to convert a very small gain into a profit the punter will consider worthwhile. That is where the preceding pages, and indeed this book as a whole, come in, with methods of selecting short-priced horses for maximum profitability discussed at several places in the text.

Also, the unfavourable position for the punter when it comes to outsiders, noted by Figgis, the Royal Commission and the rest, is not the whole story. True, the punter who shuns short-priced selections in favour of longshots is flying in the face of statistical reality. Judged from a random point of view at least, they are making things difficult for themselves.

Yet, because they are looking for a lot for a little, many punters stick to outsiders as the best hope of achieving this aim. And it is my considered opinion that they are not entirely wrong to do so.

For example, it has been shown earlier that 'instant handicapping', particularly in Flat races, will pinpoint many long-priced winners, though it is admitted that profits overall are by no means automatic and that skill and flair on the part of the punter are also needed to overcome the many losing races that go with the winners at big prices. Nevertheless, it can be done as letters I have received from readers confirm.

> *'Since buying David Duncan's book I have won £500*
> *net using his handicap system on page 24 with only*
> *20p stakes in a 'Yankee' bet which costs £2.20*
> *picking the top 3 horses by weight and the first 3 in*
> *the betting forecast. Thank you sir!'*

Thus we have two pieces of evidence from very different sources – one from a Royal Commission, one from a typical racing enthusiast, that backing horses is not a completely lost cause. Far from it. Contrary to the belief of many, it need not always be the bookmaker who wins.

An individual punter with the 'Midas touch' can win and win consistently. For the 'Midas touch' read the study of form and racing statistics. Harnessed to sound judgement and sensible staking, form is the key to the bookmaker's safe. It may not be easy, there may be many a slip along a hard road, but readers *can* acquire the 'Midas touch' from this betting manual. Part 1 has explained in great depth a logical method of studying form in general and of applying it to particular kinds of race. Part 2 will deal with racing systems which, for some, may be a similar route to at least a little of the bookmaker's cash.

PART 2

Racing Systems
to Help You Win

39
THE BEST OF THE PRESS FORM PLAN

Facts and figures are important to any serious follower of racing. For the system operator they are absolutely essential. Fortunately we have never had it so good in terms of the racing coverage offered regularly by the national press. Detailed race cards with extensive form analysis and skilfully compiled betting forecasts, course statistics plus selections by acknowledged experts are a feature of the sporting pages of every popular newspaper. Nowadays the racing fan is given so much help that winning might seem a relatively simple task.

However, it is not simple, far from it. Even with the embarrassment of riches to be found in the racing pages, the wheat still has to be sorted from the chaff. The problem of finding enough winners to yield a profit over a reasonable period of time defeats most of us.

One possible answer is to look very closely at the tips given by the racing correspondents retained by the various newspapers. They are professionals; they travel regularly to race meetings and they are paid to make a thorough study of every aspect of form. A method of betting based on their selections ought to offer a reasonably trouble-free road to success.

In fact, the typical newspaper correspondent who makes a selection in every race manages an overall ratio of approximately one winner to three losers. At first sight this may not seem too satisfactory. It is a worse average, for instance, than the general percentage of winning favourites. It must be remembered, however, that the newspaper tipster's successes include a spread of winners at all prices up to the occasional 20–1 outsider. The fact that the strike rate of winning press selections does not depend on strings of horses at short prices prompts me to suggest that in terms of potential profit they are probably the best of all readily available betting propositions.

Some backers have a favourite tipster whose selections they follow regularly. Almost everyone has a clear preference for one correspondent above all others, even if they don't always blindly follow the advice given. The BEST OF THE PRESS system recommends concentrating on the tips of ones preferred newspaper pundit. The idea, however, is not to back a selection in every race but to single out only those runners which have the highest statistical chance of winning.

One way of doing this is to examine closely the performance figures of each horse your tipster chooses. Performance figures are the record of a horse's placings on its last three outings which precedes the name of each runner on the standard race card. It is a well known fact that some three-figure combinations produce a far greater overall percentage of winners than others. Moreover the best of them show a remarkably high level of consistent success. My figures, based on many years of research for both Flat and jumps, and equally valid in handicaps and non-handicaps, are set out below. Note that there are also form figures for two-year-olds and other lightly rated animals.

Last Three Outings

011	121	321	421
101	112	122	221
311	211	114	131
111	411		

Two Career Outings Only

11	31
21	41

One Career Outing Only

1

The operating instructions for the BEST OF THE PRESS plan are very simple and require only a few minutes' work each day. Examine every selection of your chosen tipster and pick out only those which have recorded one of the above performance combinations in their most recent outings. In this way you locate up to two or three horses per day that have a double plus factor in their favour. They must be regarded as bets of the highest quality.

Nothing guarantees a profit in racing but this system has real potential for consistent success. In summer or winter you are automatically on some of the best bets your newspaper has to offer. Moreover, the selective process need not end there. The discerning backers who use their own judgement to pick and choose may be able to pinpoint one horse a day which comes close to being the perfect wager.

40
THE SPECIALITY SYSTEM

Specialisation pays or so they say. Given the right temperament, this probably applies as much to betting matters as to any other sphere of activity and this plan is to help you win bets on two-year-olds. Certainly one could do a lot worse than to concentrate on this particular aspect of the racing scene for the majority of bets. This is a great deal more sensible than jumping around from one expedient to another, clutching at every straw in the wind, always in search of the elusive big win that so seldom materialises.

To my mind two-year-olds are an excellent medium for such an approach. Competing regularly over uniform sprint distances, juveniles run to form to a remarkable degree. They are fresh and bring to their racing a zest that is all too often lacking in older horses, many of which are definitely soured by over-exposure. By contrast, consistency is the hallmark of two-year-old racing.

If you can be content with small but regular profits from fancied runners at the less spectacular end of the odds range, then it might well suit you to study the youngsters very closely. By going about it in the right way there is every chance that you could enjoy a successful season's betting with a sound capital gain at the end of the campaign to reward you for your efforts.

Two-year-olds perform within predictable limits to such an extent that a few simple tests can be used to pinpoint the best potential bets in a most effective way.

First, it is desirable that any two-year-old which carries a backer's money should have won or been placed second on its previous run. Obviously in the course of a season's racing there are plenty of examples of youngsters that were third, fourth or unplaced last time out that go on to win their next race. On the other hand, statistics show quite clearly that winners and seconds are quite outstanding. Here are the results of a survey for three full seasons:

Last Time Out	Percentage of Wins Next Outing
first/second	41 per cent
third/fourth	25 per cent
unplaced	34 per cent

When it is considered that first and seconds in the nature of things are vastly outnumbered by the others, then it is apparent that 41 is a very good percentage indeed. Clearly they offer a very high statistical chance of success.

Needless to say there are sound reasons for this excellent strike rate. Two-year-olds do reproduce their form more consistently than any other type of horse. If a youngster wins or finishes close up in a race, then unless it is asked to rise sharply in class there is every chance that it will be there or thereabouts in its next.

Over the same three-year period it was found that the win frequency for favourites in two-year-old non-handicaps (nursery handicaps were excluded because of their highly competitive nature) was 38.2 per cent and for second favourites 21.3 per cent. Note that both figures are adjusted to correct the discrepancy arising from the duplication which occurs when there are joint favourites or joint second favourites.

A combined percentage for winning first and second favourites of nearly 60 is so impressive that it seems pointless to look beyond it for the second rule of two-year-old betting. You are strongly advised to focus your attention only on the likely favourites, that is the first two in the betting forecast of a reliable sporting or daily paper.

A two-year-old, like any other thoroughbred, needs to be fully fit to do itself justice on the racecourse, However, it is standard practice among all good trainers to give their charges a periodic rest. Horses are not machines; they cannot be kept at their racing best indefinitely without a break. In this respect they are no different to human beings who go to work regularly and need a holiday from time to time in order to recharge their batteries. The surest sign that a horse has been 'let down' is a prolonged period of absence from actual competition. When it does eventually return to racing after a lay-off it may have done a good deal of work at home but there is no substitute for a gallop under racing conditions to bring a horse right up to its absolute peak.

Therefore the punter is advised to back only two-year-olds which are running within one month of their previous public outing. This is a guarantee of a horse's racing fitness and enables one to be fairly certain that no complications have developed regarding general physical well-being which might detract from its ability to reproduce its form. The third rule goes a long way to giving grounds for confidence that a horse is being backed which is fully fit and well.

The three conditions for betting in two-year-old non-handicaps may be summarised as follows:

1 Only back horses which finished first or second last time out.

2 Concentrate on the first two in the betting forecast of the newspaper used for racing purposes.

3 In no circumstances back any two-year-old which has not run in public for over a month (say 30 days).

These are rules from which no one should deviate. They will produce a short list of possibles from which to make one or more selections each racing day. The final stage in the process is left to the backer. One may feel confident enough to rely on personal reading of form or class. One may prefer to make use of the undoubted expertise of newspaper correspondents to arrive at a final choice. However, there is one guide which requires special attention. I refer to the comparative time test.

Two-year-old racing is peculiarly well suited to a close study of comparative times. Except for a minority of mile events, all juvenile races are decided over sprint distances and it is in sprints that time is of most value as an aid to finding winners. Riding tactics have little impact on calculations in races that are usually run flat out from start to finish. A two-year-old capable of recording a fast time should always be watched very closely.

Most readers will be familiar with the concept of comparative times by which each recorded race time can be classed as faster or slower than the standard for course and distance. The specialist racing press show this comparison in the following way:

Ayr	5f.	58.40s (+1.60)
Goodwood	5f.	56.50s (−0.20)
Goodwood	6f.	1/12.10s (+2.30)
Newmarket	7f.	1/26.44s (+1.94)

The vital information is contained in the brackets. Here is shown the number of seconds and tenths of a second the winner was faster (−) or slower (+) than the standard. In this way the comparative value of performances on the clock can be readily assessed even though races were run over different courses and over different distances.

Clearly from this set of figures, the horse which won or finished close up second in the Goodwood race over five furlongs where the standard was bettered by 0.20 seconds would be an obvious first choice.

There is one problem with comparative times. Races are run on different going. Obviously it is much easier to run a fast time on firm or good ground than on soft or heavy. In assessing times, therefore, some experience is needed in making an appropriate allowance for ground conditions but the time test is so valuable in evaluating two-year-old form that the effort to acquire expertise in this area is well worth making.

Looking closely at the winning times recorded by older horses on the same card is one of the best ways to evaluate the merit of a two-year-old's performance against the background of the prevailing ground conditions. If a juvenile winner or a good second did a comparative time which is close to, or even better than, the best time of the day set by an older horse, this is clearly a very sound performance. Or is the two-year-old race faster or slower against the standard than most other times recorded that afternoon? How does the two-year-old compare with a good handicapper or a selling plater, or even with a Group race winner running on the same card?

When all the racing appears very ordinary, time may be the only satisfactory key to making an accurate assessment of a piece of juvenile form. And here do not forget the draw. Were the two-year-old winner and the runner-up well drawn or badly drawn in a big field? Performances need to be upgraded or downgraded in the light of this factor. The effect of the draw should also bear on the analysis of a race currently under review. Is the fast two-year-old well or badly drawn? Check these influences out in the Racecourse Guide in Part 4. You will get a lot closer to a true estimate of the chance of a two-year-old in which you are interested.

One other factor should be considered when betting on two-year-olds. This is the time of year. The situation alters from month to month, so that a betting strategy needs to be tailored to changing circumstances very precisely. The following points should be borne in mind:

APRIL

The new season has hardly begun and most juveniles are unknown quantities. Try to find one good two-year-old bet each day and keep stakes to an absolute minimum.

MAY

Form has started to settle down but there are still plenty of youngsters who have yet to show their true potential and the going can be changeable. Stick to one bet a day with a slightly increased stake.

JUNE

By now a fairly clear picture of the new crop of two-year-olds has emerged and summer is officially here, so there should not be too many variations in going or form. Keep to a single selection but bet with confidence.

JULY AND AUGUST

Traditionally the best months of the year for the backer, July and August should bring really fast ground when short-priced horses monopolise the winner's enclosure. Now is the time to cash in with two or even three selections a day, backed in singles, doubles and trebles with one's maximum stake.

SEPTEMBER

Suddenly a lot of form becomes suspect. Classy types given plenty of time as a prelude to a three-year-old campaign at a high level appear for the first time or improve by leaps and bounds. Very likely they will upset juveniles which looked good earlier in the year. Many of the latter begin to show the effects of a long campaign, fields get more competitive and the going can change very quickly with variable weather conditions. Stakes should be dropped sharply and care must be taken not to dissipate gains from a successful spring and summer.

OCTOBER

Every horse is competing for its winter training bill, fields are huge and heavy ground plays havoc with form. Long before November comes the betting book should be closed for the year.

So a fully planned programme of two-year-old betting has been mapped out. The three basic rules should provide a small number of potential bets each day. The final process of selection gives one plenty of scope to exercise personal skill. The SPECIALITY system is thus interesting to work. In the hands of a careful operator, the system has all the prerequisites of a successful method of backing horses.

41
THE MIDSUMMER METHOD

This is a system for doubles, trebles and accumulators in selected non-handicaps.

July and August are the backer's months. Form on the Flat has had plenty of time to settle down and firm ground sees small fields and more predictable results than at any other time of the year. Favourites and near-favourites go in with monotonous regularity. The MIDSUMMER method offers a sporting chance of cashing in when circumstances are most favourable to the punter.

The general percentage of winning favourites rises sharply in every kind of race during the summer months but there are a number of categories which, according to the records, are particularly good for backers. These include maiden races for two-year-olds and non-handicaps confined to three-year-olds, of which stakes races and maidens are the two main types.

As far as two-year-old maiden races are concerned, the fact that they are restricted to non-winners means that competition is not strong. One or two horses usually stand out on what they have achieved so far and for the most part they are able to confirm their form advantage in the actual race. In this they are helped by midsummer conditions for, with the exception of mudlarks, the average thoroughbred is more reliable on fast ground than any other type of going.

Much the same reasons account for the high success rate of winning favourites in three-year-old non-handicaps. Halfway through the season on firm surfaces, the form of three-year-olds works out exceptionally well. In maiden races opposition is not strong and the fancied horses have it to themselves. Clever trainers can exploit a good three-year-old. At the smaller meetings, particularly in the north, leading yards with a monopoly of the better bred horses have a huge advantage which results in a very high percentage of winners. As for stakes races, many of these feature class horses which, almost by definition, can be expected to run to form. So three-year-olds competing on equal terms, without the intervention of the handicapper, offer relatively easy pickings for the discerning backer of favourites.

The system bet, therefore, is to back the market leaders in these types of race. As is to be expected, a very high percentage of winners may be counted upon. My statistics show a small level-stakes profit in most years. The problem is the poor odds returned on some, but by no means all the winners. The obvious solution is to back them in doubles and trebles which can be an effective way of boosting profits from short-priced selections.

The study of an old form book will prove that it is not beyond the bounds of possibility for four or five system bets to win on the same day. There is plenty of racing at this time of year, usually three meetings a day even in the middle of the week, so there are many opportunities to land successful cumulative wagers. By including accumulators whenever possible, there is every prospect of some really good payouts. One only needs to land an all-correct bet on a handful of occasions during the two-month period to be assured of a sound overall profit.

In fact bookmakers are very wary of this type of betting but multiple bets on unnamed favourites are acceptable in betting shops. Provided that one indicates that an unnamed starting price favourite is required and the time and meeting of the races involved is clearly indicated, specifying the appropriate number of doubles, trebles and accumulators with the correct stakes, there should be no trouble in getting a bet accepted. A punter taking advantage of such favourable conditions in favoured races will not be the bookmaker's ideal customer. However, any pangs of conscience should soon disappear if the backer is lucky enough to land a few really big bets.

42
THE STAR CHOICE METHOD

Many readers will be familiar with the Jockey Club's 'Pattern Race' classification by which the top non-handicaps for the various age groups are divided into Group One, Group Two, Group Three races according to their status and value. The STAR CHOICE method concentrates only on the very highest echelon of Flat racing, that is the Group One weight-for-age races run over middle distances.

Chief among these are the five Classic races – Newmarket's 2000 and 1000 Guineas, the Derby and Oaks at Epsom and finally the St Leger run at Doncaster in the autumn. Other races which fall into the elite category are four big events in July and August. They are the Eclipse Stakes (Sandown), the King George VI and Queen Elizabeth Stakes (Ascot), the Sussex Stakes (Goodwood) and the International Stakes (York). The Prince of Wales's Stakes at Royal Ascot over 10 furlongs in June and the one-mile Queen Elizabeth II Stakes on the same course in late September are two other well-established races which have recently acquired the very highest status. The Champion Stakes, decided at Newmarket near the end of the season, completes the cycle of the greatest races in the British calendar.

The STAR CHOICE approach is ultra selective and seeks to pinpoint only the best for the best. To win any one of this sequence of top races takes a horse of the highest class. Hence the basic premise of the system:

> **In such races any horse which has failed to win its last two races in similar or lesser company cannot be said to have a good chance.**

Think about this carefully. Spelled out like this the idea seems self-evident but, an examination of any of the top weight-for-age races shows how many runners can be eliminated. In the majority of cases most of the candidates fail to measure up to this standard. Yet if a horse has failed recently in inferior or even similar company, where is the confidence about it winning one of the great races which bring together the best horses from the leading stables in England, Ireland and sometimes France? If, on the other hand, we confine ourselves only to those animals which have achieved the comparatively rare feat of two recent victories in roughly the same standard of racing, then surely we have something to be on.

The STAR CHOICE method has, therefore, only one simple rule:

> **In the top weight-for-age races on the Flat, back any horse which has won both its two most recent outings, provided at least one of them was a Group One, Group Two or Group Three event.**

Group categories for big races are shown clearly in form books and in the form summaries that appear in the racing papers on the day of the race, so there should be no difficulty about determining qualifiers.

The formula will often single out only one horse for a big race. Sometimes two or three will qualify. The best advice is to back them all. Unlike most of the runners, these horses boast unbeaten form in approximately similar company. Given the prestige at stake they are sure to be trying for their lives. They are bound to go close to winning. Backing more than one in the same race is justified to make certain of being on the right horse. Part 3 explains how to back several horses in the same race at various odds for an identical profit, whichever wins.

What about starting prices? 'All odds-on', I can hear the cynics saying. Not true, for opinions always take a wide range in the great races and the prices for qualifiers can extend to 10–1 and occasionally even more. Yes, there will be short-priced favourites too but, whilst there is no such thing as a racing certainty, records show that they are in the banker class.

The STAR CHOICE system isolates only the cream of the bets in the top sphere of British racing. Look in racing annuals for past years and check the idea out. One will be agreeably surprised, not only by the number of winners from this system, but also by the odds sometimes freely available about them. It must be remembered that the performance of any racehorse, even one of the very highest class, is to some extent governed by the laws of chance but these animals definitely have unrivalled potential as betting propositions.

43
THE BARRAGE PLAN

With the aid of an old formula generally known as the BARRAGE racing system one could have backed the following two-year-old horses at Royal Ascot over just the last three years. All selections were clearly indicated without ambiguity from the betting forecast of a leading national newspaper. It was simply a case of applying a set of very simple rules.

1998

Coventry Stakes

Principal selection	RED SEA	£20 + £1.80 tax	Won 6–1	+£118.20
Danger	EMILY'S LUCK CHARM	£10 + 90p tax	Lost	–£ 10.90
				+£107.30

Queen Mary Stakes

Principal selection	BINT ALLAYL	£20 + £1.80 tax	Won 2–1	+£ 38.20
Danger	PIPALONG	£10 + 90p tax	Lost	–£ 10.90
				+£ 27.30

Norfolk Stakes

Principal selection	TOP ORDER	£20 + £1.80 tax	Lost	–£ 21.80
Danger	BUGATTI REEF	£10 + 90p tax	Lost	–£ 10.90
				–£ 32.70

Chesham Stakes

Principal selection	HISHMAH	£20 + £1.80 tax	Lost	–£ 21.80
Danger	POSTA VECCHIA	£10 + 90p tax	Lost	–£ 10.90
				–£ 32.70

Windsor Castle Stakes

Principal selection	FLANDERS	£20 + £1.80 tax	Won 15–8	+£ 35.70
Danger	SHINING DESERT	£10 + 90p tax	Lost	–£ 10.90
				+£ 24.80

Total profit from meeting: £94.00

1999

Coventry Stakes

Principal selection	FASLIYEV	£20 + £1.80 tax	Won 15–8	+£ 35.70
Danger	LINCOLN DANCER	£10 + 90p tax	Lost	–£ 10.90
				+£ 24.80

Queen Mary Stakes

Principal selection	ROWAASI	£20 + £1.80 tax	Lost	–£ 21.80
Danger	WARRIOR QUEEN	£10 + 90p tax	Lost	–£ 10.90
				–£ 32.70

Norfolk Stakes

Principal selection	WARM HEART	£20 + £1.80 tax	Won 7–2	+£ 68.20
Danger	VICTORY DAY	£10 + 90p tax	Lost	–£ 10.90
				+£ 57.30

Chesham Stakes

Principal selection	BACH	£20 + £1.80 tax	Won 5–2	+£ 18.20
Danger	HIGH WALDEN	£10 + 90p tax	Lost	–£ 10.90
				+£ 37.30

Windsor Castle Stakes

Principal selection	ROSSINI	£20 + £1.80 tax	Non-runner	—
Danger	OPTIMAITE	£10 + 90p tax	Lost	–£ 10.90
				–£ 10.90

Total profit from meeting: £75.80

2000

Coventry Stakes

Principal selection	MODIGLIANI	£20 + £1.80 tax	Lost	–£ 21.80
Danger	BRAM STOKER	£10 + 90p tax	Lost	–£ 10.90
				–£ 32.70

Queen Mary Stakes

Principal selection	DANCE ON	£20 + £1.80 tax	Lost	–£ 21.80
Danger	ROMANTIC MYTH	£10 + 90p tax	Won 4–1	+£ 39.10
				+£ 17.30

Chesham Stakes

Principal selection	CELTIC SILENCE	£20 + £1.80 tax	Won 15–8	+£ 35.70
Danger	LEOPARD SPOT	£10 + 90p tax	Lost	–£ 10.90
				+£ 24.80

Norfolk Stakes

Principal selection	SUPERSTAR LEO	£20 + £1.80 tax	Won 5–1	+£ 98.20
Danger	KEATS	£10 + 90p tax	Lost	–£ 10.90
				+£ 87.30

Windsor Castle Stakes

Principal selection	DIETRICH	£20 + £1.80 tax	Lost	−£ 21.80
Danger	PAGLIACCI	£10 + 90p tax	Lost	−£ 10.90
				−£ 32.70

Total profit from meeting: £64.00

Who did as well as this at the Royal Ascot festival in any of the three years? Perhaps, just as well, in one year but who was as successful every year? The BARRAGE system was and the plain truth is that with its aid there is an excellent chance that similar profits can be achieved in the years to come. There was no fluke about the winners pinpointed by the system.

Here are the rules:

1   Only those horses which appear in the first, second and third positions in the betting forecast of the newspaper being used for system purposes may qualify for a bet.

2   From the first three horses quoted in the betting forecast in each race, there will be two horses to back, one the principal selection with a larger stake, the other a danger selection with a smaller stake.

3   The horse with the best placing last time out of the three becomes the principal selection. Horses which did not finish first, second, third or fourth, or which have never run are all counted as 'unplaced' and rank equally. Where a horse was disqualified last time out, its original finishing position before disqualification is counted as its placing.

4   The horse with the second best placing of the three becomes the danger selection.

5   If two or more horses were identically placed last time out, the one quoted earlier in the betting forecast takes precedence.

STAKING

There is a two-points stake to win on the principal selection and one point to win on the danger selection in each of the five system races. The examples below should clarify any doubts about the exact application of the rules and cover just about all possibilities.

Position in betting forecast	Place last time out	Betting decision
1	2	Principal selection
2	0	
3	3	Danger
1	3	Danger
2	unraced	
3	2	Principal selection
1	1	Principal selection
2	1	Danger
3	2	
1	0	Principal selection
2	0	Danger
3	0	
1	4	
2=	3	Principal selection
2=	3	Danger
1	1	Principal selection
2	0	
3=	2	Danger
3=	2	
1	3	Danger
2	4	
3=	2	Principal selection
3=	1	

Note that in the last two examples, although the joint third and fourth quoted are given the same price by the forecast compiler, the fourth-named horse does not qualify for consideration, because only three horses are ever subject to examination on the score of where they finished last time out.

In the fifth example the second and third quoted are given the same price and have identical placing figures last time out, but it is the one named first which is chosen as the principal selection. The rule is always that, where there is a tie, the runner appearing first takes precedence. The third, fourth and fifth examples all illustrate this point.

The BARRAGE plan can also be applied to any two-year-old race which is not a handicap, but one needs to be selective. At big meetings later on in the season, say at York in August or Newmarket in late September, it might not be as successful as at Royal Ascot because form by then is more confused and competition possibly more intense.

If working the plan at small meetings, the recommendation is to use a series of doubles in the following way:

Two principal selections	2 pt double (one bet)
Principal selection with danger in other race	1 pt doubles (two bets)
Both dangers	1 pt double (one bet)

Total outlay: 5 pts

If races are chosen carefully, avoiding those with a likely odds-on favourite, this can be a profitable bet in the hands of a shrewd operator who can pick out races where runners outside the principal and dangers selections have little chance on form.

It is rare in racing to come across such a neat little system like the BARRAGE which consistently delivers the goods. Some readers may object to backing two horses at short prices in the same race, but the records show quite clearly that the BARRAGE plan has outstanding potential to be a steady winner.

44
THE KEY RACES METHOD

Most of the big races in the British Calendar have been established for well over a century and a half. Moreover the actual fixture list has changed little in terms of the time of year at which most important events are run. In these circumstances it is not surprising that definite patterns should have evolved which determine how horses are prepared for big races and that is the focus of this system.

Individual trainers may have their own methods of preparing horses on the gallops but season after season the big winners follow similar paths to success. These are governed by the far from limitless opportunities offered by a largely unchanging programme of meetings and races. This is the justification for the 'key race' theory of betting. In many cases the key to the results of top races is to be found in earlier races which traditionally provide important clues. It is simply a question of discovering the seasonal pattern and applying it to the current year.

Below is an analysis of the top races according to the key race idea. Allied to the study of form, it should enable you to back a lot of big winners.

THE CLASSICS

Readers are referred to the STAR CHOICE method earlier in the book, but the following is a more specific guide that may help you to choose between several possible candidates.

2000 Guineas (1m., Newmarket, early May)
Two-year-old form is frequently as important as the spring trials, but with so many top three-year-olds nowadays given a very easy time as juveniles, it is not necessarily those at the top of the two-year-old ratings which come out and run prominently in the first Classic for colts. However, the Dewhurst Stakes, over the last seven furlongs of the Rowley Mile, remains a highly significant indicator from the previous autumn. The Craven Stakes is the best three-year-old trial.

Despite all the confusion in the form which seems to attend

most modern renewals of the 2000, nearly all winners win their previous race, and the Classic itself seldom goes to a horse outside the first five or six in the betting. If a horse that was beaten last time out is to win, most likely it ran in the Craven Stakes.

1000 Guineas (1m., Newmarket, early May)
The first Classic for three-year-old fillies comes barely a month after the start of the new Flat season which is very early in the form cycle of a typical member of the equine fair sex. There are a number of trials in April which can consequently confuse the picture. The Nell Gwyn Stakes, run at Newmarket a fortnight before the Classic, has proved highly misleading in recent times, and the Fred Darling Stakes at Newbury may be a better guide. On the other hand there are plenty of examples in the record book of a filly succeeding first time out in the big race.

Two-year-old form, therefore, is very much the key. One of the leading half-dozen fillies in the 'International Classification of Two-Year-Olds' form a group which often includes the winner. Most French-trained winners of the race have also won the Prix Imprudence at Longchamp in April. Top fillies occasionally cross the Irish Sea for the race; their chance should never be lightly dismissed.

Oaks Stakes (1½m., Epsom, early June)
Winners of the 1000 Guineas have a good record and placed horses from the Newmarket Classic also do well, although in an age of specialisation fewer fillies challenge for both races than used to be the case. Leaving aside the Newmarket form, the Oaks often falls to a filly which has won well over a mile and a half and is preferably unbeaten at three-years-old. Once in a while the race goes to a very lightly raced filly from a top yard. Favourites only win in their turn.

Derby Stakes (1½m., Epsom, early June)
The Derby is an international event featuring challengers from England, Ireland and France. There are many trials but no one race consistently provides the best clue. The race is seldom won by anything but a genuine stayer. Hence the failure in the race of so many 2000 Guineas winners whose speed is often blunted by the extra four furlongs.

Favourites or near-favourites dominate the race, so look for a well-backed candidate which has won at or close to a mile-and-a-half in top company. This usually cuts the field down to a few live contenders from which the winner may come. An interesting feature in recent times has been the number of winners which were given an easy time at two. Top class two-year-old form is, therefore, no longer a necessary credential, as was once the case.

St Leger (1¾m., Doncaster, early September)
Nowadays winners of the race take many routes to Classic glory, and races such as the Derby, Irish Derby and Great Voltigeur Stakes at York have seen their influence diminish over the years, with many St Leger winners emerging late in their second season from outside the ranks of the established stars. Nevertheless, the race has become very much one for favourites. If opposing the favourite bet each-way, for fields seldom get much above double figures and one could 'steal' a win as well as the inflated place money if the market leader goes down at a short price.

WEIGHT-FOR-AGE AND CONDITION RACES

Ormonde Stakes (1m. 5f., Chester, early May)
This important early season test for senior horses seldom falls to anything but a form horse. If one of the first three in either the previous season's Derby or St Leger contests the race, then this should be something of a banker bet.

Coronation Cup (1½m., Epsom, early June)
Epsom's big middle-distance event used to be dominated by Classic winners of the previous year but nowadays with so many good horses retiring to stud at the end of their three-year-old season, the race usually goes to one of the second eleven. The Jockey Club Stakes at the Newmarket Guineas meeting is probably the best single 'key' race. French raiders should be noted, especially if the home side appears to lack quality.

Queen Anne Stakes (1m., Ascot, mid-June)
The Lockinge Stakes at Newbury is an important 'key race' for this tough contest which produces winners at all kinds of prices.

St James's Palace Stakes (1m., Ascot, mid-June)
One of Royal Ascot's showpieces, the race often goes to a horse with win-or-place form in the Craven Stakes or the 2000 Guineas. The winner of the Irish 2000 Guineas must also be considered if contesting the race. Runners from France are not all that frequent but they have an above-average record if already established as one of the top French milers. This is definitely not a favourite's race; most winners come from the middle order of the betting.

Prince of Wales's Stakes (1¼m., Ascot, mid-June)
Now a Group One championship race, it seldom falls to a horse outside the first two in the market.

Coronation Stakes (1m., Ascot, mid-June)
The race often crowns the achievements of a winner of the Irish 1000 Guineas, or is a consolation prize for a filly which ran well in the English 1000. The race has Group One status, however, and a late-developing filly can sometimes shock established stars. Given the right material, the big guns among the Newmarket training elite make a speciality of this.

Lancashire Oaks (1½m., Haydock, early July)
Now open to four-year-olds, the race is still on the agenda of the Epsom Oaks' failures. Any filly which finished in the first half dozen at Epsom should go close.

Eclipse Stakes (1¼m., Sandown, early July)
This is a race of the very highest class open to three-year-olds and upwards over 10 furlongs. Milers as well as 12-furlong horses can win if they have the class. It takes a real top-notcher to succeed in the race, and nearly all winners have at least one Group race victory to their credit during the current season, with many having been also, at least, placed in a Classic either this year or last. The record of favourites, however, is only average. The Prince of Wales's Stakes at Ascot has been the best single guide.

King George VI and Queen Elizabeth Stakes (1½m., Ascot, late July)
Above-average winners of the Epsom and Irish Derbys often win but only if they have the overall form to suggest that their Derby win was not a one-off. But winners of the Eclipse Stakes, though stepping up in distance, often have a vital edge in speed on going that is usually fast. Three-year-olds have by far the best record for it appears that the scale of weight-for-age favours them at this time of year.

Sussex Stakes (1m., Goodwood, August)
Three-year-olds dominate this showdown between the best milers at Glorious Goodwood. The St James's Palace Stakes may have a bearing, and Royal Ascot form generally comes out on top. The first three in the betting have a virtual monopoly of results, though it may not be easy to pick the right one.

International Stakes (1¼m., York, mid-August)
Now established in the very top echelon of racing, York's big test used to provide consolation for horses that ran well in the Epsom Derby. But, in recent times all three-year-olds seem to struggle against the best older horses. Favourites do badly and outsiders win far more often than is usual in a Group One contest. Not a race on which to 'go for broke'.

Yorkshire Oaks (1½m., York, mid-August)
The form of the top staying fillies has moved on a bit since the beginning of June so that, whereas the Epsom Oaks does still sometimes give a clue, later races such as the Ribblesdale Stakes at Royal Ascot, the Nassau Stakes at Goodwood and in particular the Irish Oaks at the Curragh are more likely to provide the answer.

Park Hill Stakes (1¾m., Doncaster, early September)
Known as the 'fillies' St Leger' and run over the full Classic distance, the race has become much less important in recent years. Classic fillies seldom appear nowadays, and the race usually goes to an improving sort from a top English yard. The ability to stay, as established by the racecourse test or, failing that, a staying pedigree, is the vital form factor to look for in a probable winner.

Queen Elizabeth II Stakes (1m., Ascot, late September)
This is now a world-class race and the winner will usually take the title of 'champion miler'. Anything less than top-class form should be disregarded. However, the presumed 'good thing' frequently gets turned over. Three-year-olds seem to have the edge over older horses.

Champion Stakes (1¼m., Newmarket, mid-October)
Run over the straight ten furlongs at Newmarket in the autumn when even some of the best horses have had enough for the season, this prestigious weight-for-age race is one of the trickiest in the calendar. An English Classic winner, either a three- or four-year-old, and not necessarily the one at the shortest price, is often the best solution. Fillies are at their peak at this time of year and they have an outstanding record. French raiders sometimes win at a very good price.

THE CUP RACES

Gold Cup (2½m., Ascot, mid-June)
In an age of speed very few horses are able to produce top-class acceleration at the end of a marathon distance. Those that possess this rare quality will nearly always have established their reputation and will start as a hot favourite. They usually win. In an average year, however, with no outstanding horse in the field, the way is open for unfancied horses to overturn a weak favourite.

Form is hard to assess because of the extreme distance. Breeding is often a better guide. Look for a tough, staying sire, with plenty of stamina close up on the dam's side. The Henry II Stakes at Sandown in May is the best single trial. The Prix du Cadran, the French equivalent of the Gold Cup, sometimes throws up a challenger but French predominance in staying races is very old history. An outstanding French raider apart, it usually pays to stick with the home side.

Goodwood Cup (2m., Goodwood, August)
An obvious choice is the Gold Cup winner if that horse contests the race but the price is bound to be short. The race used to be run over five furlongs further. The reduction in distance has produced more

competitive fields, but form is that much more reliable. Do not look beyond the first three in the betting but, remember that Goodwood is a course for specialists. Tough, older stayers often beat off the challenge of young pretenders.

Doncaster Cup (2¼m., Doncaster, early September)
This is very definitely a favourites' race. Winners of the Yorkshire Cup, Ascot's Sagaro Stakes, the Henry II Stakes or the Goodwood Cup which occupy the leading position in the market ought to be something of a banker bet. The Gold Cup form, by contrast, is not always upheld on Town Moor.

Jockey Club Cup (2m., Newmarket, mid-October)
Fields are small. Yet prices are, relatively speaking, often generous. If form indicates a reasonably certain winner the result is likely to confirm the analysis and pay a handsome dividend. The horse with the best credentials usually wins at more than fair odds.

TOP SPRINTS

King's Stand Stakes (5f., Ascot, mid-June)
This big sprint has seen the monopoly of three-year-olds broken in recent years. More important than age, a victory in at least one Group race during the current season is a useful qualification. The Temple Stakes at Sandown remains the best single trial, as it has been for many, many years. The Duke of York Stakes, too, though over a furlong more, can provide a sound 'key' from York's big May meeting.

July Cup (6f., Newmarket, early July)
This is a very hot race these days and it often pays to stick with the two traditional guides, the Cork and Orrery Stakes and the King's Stand Stakes, both run at Royal Ascot. The French challenge only occasionally, but if a runner from across the Channel is in the field, the hint should be taken. Horses of all ages win.

Nunthorpe Stakes (5f., York, mid-August)
The market is not always a good guide and the 'key race' picture is confused. The state of the ground is often the deciding factor. A

horse needs the going to be exactly to its liking if it is to have that split-second edge over other flying machines. Check out the form book and the stallion guide on pages 54–6.

Haydock Sprint Cup (6f., Haydock, mid-September)
Here too the ground is often decisive among sprinters that are very close on form. Outsiders seldom win but actual favourites do not have a particularly good record either.

Diadem Stakes (6f., Ascot, late-September)
The race is often run on heavy ground, and the going is frequently the deciding factor. Most winners have won at least one race in Group Three or better.

BIG HANDICAPS

Lincoln Handicap (1m., Doncaster, late March)
Much depends on the draw in the season's first big handicap, so small stakes are advised. Fitness is the key with most runners making their seasonal debut. Look for those horses which have shown that they come to hand early by winning in the first month of the previous season. Live candidates should also have good win-and-place form in fair handicap company at the back-end to have a real chance of success in this highly competitive race. Recent form on the all-weather can also confer a decisive advantage.

Chester Cup (2¼m., Chester, early May)
Run round Chester's tight turns, the race is not so much a test of bottomless stamina as it might first appear. Just as important is a top-class jockey who can judge the pace on the tricky track. Horses that have already recorded a win in the first weeks of the season should be noted. For a big handicap, most winners are surprisingly well fancied.

Royal Hunt Cup (1m., Ascot, mid-June)
There are numerous good mile handicaps in the weeks leading up to Ascot's annual cavalry charge, so there are no obvious key races that can be singled out. Not a race for outright favourites but the winner nearly always comes from the first half-dozen in the

betting. Big stables tend to monopolise the race and the small trainer is seldom able to make an impact.

Wokingham Handicap (6f., Ascot, mid-June)
One of the most open handicaps of the year, this big sprint is another race where heavy betting is asking for trouble. There is no really reliable single 'key race' but, strangely for a sprint, high-weighted horses fare badly on the whole.

Northumberland Plate (2m., Newcastle, late June)
The 'Pitman's Derby', as the race is known, usually falls to a well-backed candidate. The Queen's Prize at Kempton in mid-April, the Chester Cup and the Ascot Handicap at the Royal meeting are three races for stayers that can give useful hints.

Stewards' Cup (6f., Goodwood, late July)
There is no key formula to the race with winners coming from many directions. However, two factors are most important. Three-year-olds are just coming into their own against older horses at this time of year and this age group should be examined as closely as any other. Also, a good draw is a virtual necessity for success. The old bias in favour of high numbers may have gone due to recent course alterations, but a position on either fence is a definite plus. Horses drawn in the middle of the field are likely to struggle.

Ebor Handicap (1¾m., York, mid-August)
There are no easy solutions to this most open of staying handicaps. The class of the race is always very high, so lightweights are up against it, save for the unexposed three-year-old which might just fool the handicapper. Valuable staying handicaps at Newmarket, Ascot and Goodwood are the best guides.

Ayr Gold Cup (6f., Ayr, late September)
An each-way bet on horses in the first three in the Portland Handicap at Doncaster's big September meeting often pays a dividend in the Ayr race. Outsiders rarely win; well-backed horses (up to 14–1) with or without good recent form often do.

Cambridgeshire (1m. 1f., Newmarket, early October)
This is usually the most difficult handicap of the year. Horses which finished in the first four in the Royal Hunt Cup represent good value and can win at a big price. Among the market leaders, look out for a horse which has suddenly begun to improve dramatically in the last month or so.

Cesarewitch (2¼m., Newmarket, mid-October)
Great reserves of stamina are needed for this end-of-season marathon. Many winners are either established stayers with a biggish weight to match their form or improving three-year-olds down at the bottom of the handicap. Form is hard to assess for a race over such a long distance but note very carefully the entries of 'clever' trainers who like to bet. Well-backed horses generally do well.

BIG RACES OVER JUMPS

Thomas Pink Gold Cup Handicap Chase (2m. 4½f., Cheltenham, mid-November)
The first big race of the jumping year is over an extended two and a half miles, and many of the best handicappers at this 'in-between' distance contest the prize. Though there are exceptions, genuine two- or three-milers are probably running in the wrong race. Most winners have had a preparatory race in the current season but this is not essential. A win, or at least a good place last time out, is desirable as evidence that a horse is capable of going on to win such a competitive event. Look for a 'class' horse carrying 11st or more, or a lightweight with excellent form figures. Ten-year-olds or over are best forgotten in a race for up-and-coming young chasers. Outright favourites and rank outsiders are suspect; the first four or five in the betting are statistically favoured.

Hennessy Cognac Gold Cup Handicap Chase (3m. 2½f., Newbury, late November)
Most winners have at least one warm-up race, and quite a few have two or more. Top trainers 'farm' the race, and the smaller handler is bound to struggle in the face of competition from the big yards. Despite the wide difference in race distance, the Thomas Pink Gold

Cup is frequently a reliable guide. Favourites do far better than might be expected in such a keenly contested handicap, and the middle rank in the betting dominates when the actual market leader fails to pull it off.

King George VI Chase (3m., Kempton, late December)
The cream of the chasing ranks is on show in the premier mid-season jumping prize but the race does seem to require special talents, perhaps because speed is at a premium over Kempton's easy three miles. Horses frequently win in consecutive years. The previous season's Cheltenham Gold Cup is rarely a good guide – Cheltenham is a very different course to Kempton. Favourites do well, often at a generous price.

Racing Post Handicap Chase (3m., Kempton, late February)
Though a handicap, a horse with a touch of class is needed for this hotly contested race. Therefore, ignore lightweights and outsiders.

Champion Hurdle (2m., Cheltenham, mid-March)
Two or more victories by the same horse has always been a feature of the history of hurdling's crown. Also, most horses beaten one year are not very likely to win the next. Concentrate on young horses if you think there will be a new champion. The prices of winning favourites tend to be poor in a race where heavy gamblers tend to 'get stuck in' on a presumed 'certainty'. However, there is plenty of each-way value, and this is often the best bet in the race for the average punter.

Queen Mother Champion Chase (2m., Cheltenham, mid-March)
In what is very much a race for specialists over the minimum trip, previous winners often retain their crown. Failing that, last year's second or third nearly always win or go close. Avoid very young and old horses; nine- and ten-year-olds have the best record. Keep to the first three in the betting.

Cheltenham Gold Cup Chase (3m. 2½f., Cheltenham, mid-March)
Top-class conditions races are the best guide. Handicap form, however impressive on the surface, should be left severely alone. An

animal needs to be at its absolute peak to win, so veterans of over ten years old have little chance. Most years it pays to keep to the first four or five in the betting but the favourite itself, though often at generous odds, has little going for it if judged by the recent history of the race.

Grand National Handicap Chase (4½m., Aintree, early April)
Stamina and jumping ability are the vital ingredients for Aintree's spectacular. Form, therefore, is the key to the race despite its formidable reputation for thrills and spills. Animals carrying nearer 12 st. than 11 st. are at a serious disadvantage over such testing jumping country and an extreme distance. Conversely, minimum weight is 10 st. Few horses set to carry more than their long handicap weight (see specialist press) have the class to succeed.

Horses of all ages win, and advancing years have never prevented the right horse from claiming the prize. The betting market is the most consistent pointer of all. Despite the occasional winning outsider, well-backed horses, sometimes without obvious form claims, monopolise the record of results. No horse can win unless it completes the course however, and finding the winner in a single selection is a difficult task.

The key race theory is not just hindsight. If you try it out, you will be amazed how often history repeats itself. There will, inevitably, be failures but the statistical record is there for those who wish to use it to their advantage.

45
THE BLUEPRINT METHOD

When winter comes most punters turn to favourites as the likeliest source of a regular flow of winners. This is perfectly understandable. Despite the fact that National Hunt racing has become increasingly competitive in the last couple of decades, jumping favourites retain a remarkably high level of consistency. However, one still has to pick the right favourites.

The problem has exercised some of the most ingenious minds in racing over the years and a number of suggestions have been put forward for providing automatic selections. Below I show an analysis of some of the most sensible of these. In each case a one-year cycle of National Hunt racing has been used as a yardstick.

	Winning percentage	Average annual profit (+) or loss (−)
Longest distance chase of the day (including handicaps)	38.6%	−1 pt
Most valuable chase of the day (including handicaps)	39.7%	+2 pts
First non-handicap on the card (principal meeting)	38.6%	−10 pts
Last race on the card (principal meeting)	37.8%	−9 pts
Favourite quoted at the second shortest price in the betting forecast of all favourites (all meetings)	54.1%	+13 pts

It can be seen that some of these methods are fundamentally sound. Yet a seasonal profit which only just exceeds double figures, or not even that, is a poor reward for a period of betting that runs from November to March. On the other hand, the general winning percentages are quite encouraging. Clearly discrimination will pay and the following series of guidelines is designed to separate the good bets from the bad. First, however, I show a set of statistics which complete the picture about jumping favourites backed overall with no attempt at selectivity.

	Winning percentage	Average annual profit (+) or loss (−)
All non-handicap chases	39.2%	−19 pts
All non-handicap hurdles	40.6%	−8 pts
Novice chases (non-handicaps)	47.5%	−2 pts
Novice hurdles (non-handicaps)	41.7%	−7 pts
Best race on the card (5th)	39.6%	+2 pts
Worst race on the card (3rd)	31.2%	−17 pts

The two sets of figures given in this section should serve as the basis of calculations but obviously it is necessary to pick and choose. In fact there are a number of factors whose worth cannot always be demonstrated in statistical terms but which long experience has taught me must cut out many poor bets. Combined with the full analysis of jumping favourites set out above, they can only help to increase the ratio of winners to losers.

1 Back only favourites that were first or second last time out. There are plenty of false favourites even over the sticks. This simple rule ensures backing animals with a basic form qualification that many market choices do not have.

2 If it is decided to back a favourite in a handicap, stick to small fields. I would make it an absolute rule not to bet in a handicap with more than ten runners. 'The bigger the field, the bigger the certainty' is perhaps the silliest of all racing maxims. Even in non-handicaps chances are increased mathematically in small fields.

3 Most bets should be on horses running within 14 days of their previous run. As many as 51.2 per cent of all winners over jumps had this qualification in a survey of 500 races specially undertaken to establish the statistical facts about recent form.

Conversely, only 10.5 per cent of winners had been off the track for 29 or more days. Even if the '14-day rule' is not strictly kept, one must avoid any runner which has not had a public outing for over a month.

This completes the guide to backing favourites in winter, which is a BLUEPRINT of all possibilities. The message behind everything that has been said is that it is absolutely vital to be selective.

Personally I am impressed by the high percentage of winning favourites in novice chases nowadays. Quite obviously there has been an important change on the jumping scene in this respect. There was a time when novice hurdles were a superior betting medium for followers of short-priced horses. However, the introduction of a system of penalties has made it more difficult for a good novice to win strings of consecutive hurdle races and the winning percentage of favourites has declined as a result.

Horses in their first chasing season, on the other hand, appear to be much better schooled than once was the case. Though the traditional wisdom that it is risky to back unexposed animals over fences remains an important caveat when assessing the form of individual horses, the *overall* percentage of winning favourites and the *overall* record of only a tiny loss at level stakes seem to belie the old notions about novice chasers.

Novice chases are seldom very competitive and if a favourite at fair odds against can be found that ran first or second last time out and which is trained by one of the dozen or so leading National Hunt trainers, then there is definitely something to bet on. But if on a given day there is no horse which fulfils these conditions, then the BLUEPRINT should be used to select an outstanding prospect in another category of race. Everything depends on what material is available at the time. Sometimes it is not possible to find even one favourite which can be backed with real confidence. In that case do not bet. In other words, discriminating betting pays; betting for betting's sake most certainly does not.

Those who like an automatic system bet on favourites might like to try the following method for jumps, based on some of the conclusions of the BLUEPRINT combined with the 'best races for favourites' feature in the RACECOURSE GUIDE. Here follows a dozen courses for hunter chases and a dozen for novice chases, all with a very high incidence of winning favourites statistically, and good potential for profit at level stakes for the kind of race specified.

Hunter Chases	Novice Chases
Aintree	Cartmel
Ascot	Chepstow
Ayr	Exeter
Bangor-on-Dee	Fakenham
Cheltenham	Folkestone
Kelso	Huntingdon
Ludlow	Newcastle
Newbury	Newton Abbot
Perth	Plumpton
Sandown Park	Sedgefield
Stratford	Wincanton
Towcester	Worcester

The hunter chase season does not start until January of each year, and novice chase form has largely settled down by New Year. Therefore the recommendation is to bet on the unnamed favourites from both lists during the period from 1 January to 31 May inclusive. During these five months it is rare to have to make more than one bet a day which is the ideal scenario for the application of a sound staking plan, and in particular one that is able to exploit a very high percentage of winners.

The recommended system is the one usually called *Reverse Labouchère*, and is better known in the world of roulette. Applied to the right kind of horse racing however, it can produce some very fine profit figures over relatively short periods of betting, such as the five months of betting operations advised here.

Its rules are:

1   Write down a series of consecutive numbers from 1 upwards. For our system bet on hunters and novices 1 2 3 4 5 6 7 will be best. This 'line' is the initial determinant of stakes and is subsequently adjusted after each bet.

2   Always stake the sum of the first and last number in the line. Cross these off after a loser, but add the winning stake to the end of the line after a winner.

3   If all the numbers in a line are completely crossed off, start a new line of 1 to 7.

Here is an incomplete example of some bets using the system. It should make the meaning of the rules absolutely clear.

REVERSE LABOUCHÈRE STAKING SYSTEM

Line	Stake	Result	Total Profit (+) or Loss (−)
1 2 3 4 5 6 7	£8.00	Lost	−£ 8.00
~~1~~ 2 3 4 5 6 ~~7~~	£8.00	Lost	−£16.00
~~2~~ 3 4 5 ~~6~~	£8.00	Won 7–4	−£ 2.00
3 4 5 8	£11.00	Won evens	+£9.00
3 4 5 8 11	£14.00	Won 8–11	+£19.22
3 4 5 8 11 14	£17.00	Won 6–4	+£44.72
3 4 5 8 11 14 17	£20.00	Lost	+£24.72
~~3~~ 4 5 8 11 14 ~~17~~	£18.00	Won 2–5	+£36.92
4 5 8 11 14 18	£22.00	Won 11 8	+£62.28
4 5 8 11 14 18 22	£26.00	Won 5–6	+£83.86
4 5 8 11 14 18 22 26	£30.00	Lost	+£53.86
~~4~~ 5 8 11 14 18 22 ~~26~~	£27.00		

Note that for simplicity's sake all bets are shown without betting tax.

The general effect of the system rules is that stakes will rise quite sharply on a run of winners, but are reduced fairly gradually when losers are encountered, thus limiting losses.

On a long sequence of winners, even one interspersed with a few losers, profits can spiral dramatically but equally, stakes can get very high, thereby incurring the risk of dissipating accrued gains on a run of losers. Therefore one is advised to 'check out' after a certain profit target is reached. On an opening stake of £8 it might well be possible to take profits from a 'bank' that has reached £150. One could then begin again with a new line of 1 2 3 4 5 6 7. If things continue to go well, another decent profit can be built up quickly, and there is no risk of losing all that has been achieved by a long sequence in which losers predominate over winners.

On a brilliant but by no means impossible run of success, the *Reverse Labouchère* formula could reach profits of as much of four figures over a reasonably extended period. There is, however, the commensurate risk of a sudden and dramatic fall from the heights if a very bad sequence of results were to set in. Operating the system without a predetermined profit target is for out-and-out gamblers only. So the staking method calls for shrewd money management, and it should be tested out on some imaginary sequences of reasonable length in order to appreciate both its advantages and dangers.

A final point is that on the few occasions where one gets two selections on the same day, back only one of them unless one is in a betting shop and therefore in a position to adjust the stake according to the formula after the first runner. Otherwise make one clear selection by taking, say, the horse quoted at the shorter price in the betting forecast. Any other action risks disturbing the rhythm of the staking plan. Similarly, in the highly unlikely event of there being three qualifiers on the same day, it is better to back one horse with the correct stake than to make a set of approximations which can only match the requirements of the formula if one is able to bet from race to race.

Automatic systems of the above kind are not to everyone's liking and in any case the hunter chase/novice chase method is only for five months of the year. But, using the BLUEPRINT wisely and well at all times during the jumping season could achieve a percentage of winners to surprise and delight any backer.

46
THE VALUE FOR MONEY JUMPING SYSTEM

Racing systems are usually based on either favourites or outsiders. In a favourites system the backer hopes that a high percentage of winners will yield enough gains to offset the cost of losers and the imposition of betting tax. Thus if 100 horses are backed at an average price of 6–4, with tax paid on stakes, something over 40 must win for the backer to break even and absorb the betting levy. A greater number of winners produce a profit. How much profit will depend on how many more than 40 per cent eventually win.

In an outsiders' system on the other hand, the calculation is, of necessity, less precise. The backer now chooses horses likely to go off at a much wider range of prices which together represent 'long odds', knowing full well that racing being the sport it is, most of them will be beaten. The hope here is that just a few outsiders will win to pay for the losers and still produce a profit after tax. Typical of this sort of system is the old favourite of choosing 12 handicappers to follow at the beginning of the season and backing them through thick and thin for the rest of the year. If the horses selected fulfil expectations, a win or two for all, or nearly all, of them when starting at much better than average odds will cancel out the inevitable losers and produce an overall surplus from all the bets made during the season. There are other examples of systems for outsiders, but the '12 to follow' method exemplifies the principle underlying most of them.

Which is the better way to bet? Part of the answer to this question is that it is very much a matter of the individual punter's temperament. Some people need the reassurance of a reasonably steady flow of winners regardless of starting prices. Others are more sanguine and are able to bide their time until the big winners materialise.

Another approach is to deliberately choose a method of selection that is likely to throw up a varied mixture of horses in terms of starting prices, perhaps from odds-on chances through the middle order of the betting right up to the outsider category of runner. In my experience such methods are almost by definition unreliable and should be avoided. They cannot really be based on any consistent, logical principle of form, and the chaotic nature of selections must be reflected in a ragbag of results.

There is, however, a fourth way, and this is to deliberately target horses in the middle range of the betting market. That is the idea incorporated in the VALUE FOR MONEY system explained in this chapter. As we saw in Part 1, surveys by various authorities reveal that purely random betting on horses in this middle range will lose more than backing favourites at random, but a lot less than will be lost by focusing only on longshots. However, this is not the whole story.

If the random principle is replaced by logical form criteria, there is every chance that random losses from medium-priced horses can be converted into a sound overall gain. Suppose, by way of example, the backer finds a series of horses all starting at 4–1. Only one winner in four or 25 per cent is needed to break even before tax, and an average of between one and two winners in four will yield a profit that would certainly be acceptable over a period of time. Such a theoretical target does not seem unreasonable in practice given the use of methods of selection designed to single out only quality choices with a well-above average chance of succeeding. Or put another way – if medium-priced horses can be found with form credentials at least as good as runners at shorter prices – then the former must represent 'value for money' and offer real potential for worthwhile profits.

The complete VALUE FOR MONEY formula uses a set of criteria that will guarantee such form credentials and apply them in races where the middle rank in the betting is known to do well. Therefore, there will be little prospect of very short-priced favourites or big outsiders spoiling the party.

The VALUE FOR MONEY rules are as follows:

1   Bet only in handicap chases of ten or fewer runners.

2   To qualify for a bet a horse must have won last time out during the current season.

3   The horse must be top-rated in the race ratings of the newspaper used for betting purposes.

4 The horse must be second or third favourite in the betting forecast of the same newspaper.

Personally I use Formcast who provides the 'spot' horse of the *Daily Mail*, and who is surely the leader among the Fleet Street journalists at work in the field of private handicapping. A preference for a different handicapper or some other race ratings in another newspaper is the reader's prerogative.

Some may prefer to include favourites as well as second and third favourites in the scheme. There will certainly be a lot more qualifiers and more winners. But there will also be a lot more losers.

What is important is to follow the rules on a consistent basis and stick to the same race ratings throughout. As they stand, without any modification, the four factors combined in the above rules together provide a rock-solid foundation for finding winners from one area of the odds range in a particular kind of race. As we have seen in Part 1, in the section on instant handicapping for jumps, handicap chases provide ideal material for finding the sort of winner defined in and envisaged by the rules.

There will not be all that many system qualifiers even during the whole length of the National Hunt season 'proper' which, for our betting purposes, starts from the Monday after the Flat's St Leger and ends on the last Saturday in April the following year. It may be, however, that they will be well worth waiting for.

47
THE MULTI-LINK STAKING FORMULA

Although assured of plenty of winners, the confirmed favourite backer faces the constant problem of converting short-priced successes into a worthwhile profit. The MULTI-LINK method of staking is one of the best systems ever devised for solving the difficulty.

Stakes are on single daily selections but the formula links up a series of doubles spread over several days in order to make the very best use of those winners that are backed. Moreover, the maximum number of points at risk in any one week is known in advance. It is always 15.

The 15 points which cover one bet a day for a full six-day week are divided up as follows:

$$5 \quad 4 \quad 3 \quad 2 \quad 1 \quad 0$$

These basic daily units increase according to winners backed but, if the first five bets lose, then no double has materialised, so there would be no bet on Saturday.

On Monday the bet is always five points. After each winner combine the odds (3–1 = 3 + 1 = 4, 6–4 = 1½ + 1 = 2½, 4–7 = ⁴⁄₇ + 1 = 1⁴⁄₇ i.e. 1.57, and so on). Now add the resultant figure to each of the basic units for the remaining days including Saturday.

As an example suppose the first bet wins at 3–1. Then the remaining bets for the week would each be increased by four points (3 + 1) to get:

4	3	2	1	0
4	4	4	4	4
8	7	6	5	4

The second and third bets lost but on Thursday there is a 2–1 winner. As a result the stakes for Friday and Saturday become:

5	4
3	3
8	7

Friday's selection is a loser but on Saturday a winner is backed at 6–4, so the stakes and results for the six-day cycle have been:

Stakes:	5	8	7	6	8	7		
Results:	3–1	L	L	2–1	L	6–4		
Gains:	15			12		10½	=	37½ pts
Losses:		8	7		8		=	23 pts
						Overall profit	=	14½ pts

Now if the 15 points had been invested at level stakes of 2½ points for each of the six days, the profit on this sequence would have amounted to only 8¾ points.

In other words, provided one can be reasonably confident of picking around 50 per cent winning favourites each week, then the MULTI-LINK formula should increase gains when compared with level-stakes betting on the same sequence.

There is, however, betting tax to consider. This has been omitted from the examples of the system in action to keep the mathematics as straightforward and comprehensible as possible. Unfortunately, away from the racecourse we all have to pay the levy. If one is confident of regularly picking enough winners to allow the MULTI-LINK method to achieve its goal of a good profit from a reasonable incidence of winners at very ordinary starting prices, then the bullet should be bitten and the tax paid on stakes. Payment is disproportionately more if the bookmaker deducts duty from a series of winning doubles.

Also, as with practically everything connected with betting on horses, there are drawbacks other than the necessity to contribute to the sport by way of betting tax. It is only fair to admit that the formula loses against level stakes if:

a) only one winner in a week is backed – the principle of linked doubles to boost profits fails to operate;
b) two or even three winners at very short odds, all odds-on or close to it are backed – level stakes do better by a slight margin.

In all other cases the formula scores and often quite handsomely.

If habitually backing a lot of horses at odds-on, the *Reverse Labouchère* method given as part of the National Hunt

BLUEPRINT is preferable to the MULTI-LINK. *Reverse Labouchère* actually requires plenty of very short-priced horses that will yield a high percentage of winners, so that strings of successes can boost gains quickly and out of all proportion to the initial stakes. MULTI-LINK, on the other hand, is a much gentler progression. It should be used for selections at the kind of prices shown in our examples, even if the strike rate of winners is sacrificed, at least in part, to find horses at reasonable odds.

For example, examine this sequence of bets. Prices are far from exceptional, but most are at odds against. That is enough to produce a healthy plus in favour of the MULTI-LINK formula over level-stakes betting:

	Basic Units		
Monday	5		
Tuesday	4		
Wednesday	3	$+3\frac{1}{2}$	= £6.50
Thursday	2	$+3\frac{1}{2} + 2\frac{3}{4}$	= £8.25
Friday	1	$+3\frac{1}{2} + 2\frac{3}{4}$	= £7.25
Saturday	0	$+3\frac{1}{2} + 2\frac{3}{4} + 1\frac{8}{13}$	= £7.87

	Stakes	Result	Profit or loss
Monday	£5.00	Lost	−£ 5.00
Tuesday	£4.00	Won 5–2	+£10.00
Wednesday	£6.50	Won 7–4	+£11.38
Thursday	£8.25	Lost	−£ 8.25
Friday	£7.25	Won 8–13	+£ 4.50
Saturday	£7.87	Won 5–4	+£ 9.84

'MULTI-LINK' profit = £22.47

Level-stakes (£2.50) profit = £10.31

The MULTI-LINK Formula was originally conceived as a series of double events arising from a single daily selection from Monday to Saturday. However, if it is felt that on a particular day there is no worthwhile wager, the system can still be used. Provided it is applied to six consecutive selections on different days, the mathematical symmetry of the formula is retained. If the preference is not to bet every day it is simpler to think of it in terms of six bets and not in terms of days of the week thus:

Bet 1	Bet 2	Bet 3	Bet 4	Bet 5	Bet 6
5	4	3	2	1	0

This might represent a series of wagers spread as follows:

Bet 1	Bet 2	Bet 3
Monday	Wednesday	Friday
5	4	3

Bet 4	Bet 5	Bet 6
Saturday	Tuesday	Thursday
2	1	0

Moreover, if departing in this way from the strict Monday to Saturday rota, there is no need to miss a good wager on the sixth day should the first five in the series prove unsuccessful. Suppose Bets 1 to 5 lost in the above example. In that event the selection for Thursday could become Bet 1 with a 5-point stake in a new series of six bets.

This method of numbering the bets 1 to 6, rather than labelling them Monday to Saturday, can also be used to accommodate Sunday racing, where Sunday would be the first bet in a new sequence if six bets had been made in the week so far, from Monday onwards. It could also be some other number in the sequence if not betting every day. The important thing is to calculate stakes from a rota comprising bets 1 to 6, whatever days of the week they happen to fall on.

In the case of a mathematical formula of this kind a great deal depends on prices in relation to the number of winners and losers. But if you are the kind of backer who finds it relatively easy to pick out one good thing a day, then MULTI-LINK is for you. You need to avoid strings of odds-on chances for the formula to do its work but it will always increase profits compared with level stakes on a turnover of winners at reasonable prices.

48
THE COUNTERPOISE PLAN

In most staking plans the backer is required to increase stakes on a series of losers. An eventual winner, it is hoped, will pay off losses to date and still yield a profit. Frequently, however, too long a losing run and a winner at too short a price combine to defeat the idea. The sequence reaches the point where the chance of recovering losses, still less of showing a gain, finally disappears. With the COUNTERPOISE method – a unique way of betting from Monday to Saturday – stakes gradually diminish while prices increase. In this way it overcomes the fundamental deficiencies of the usual type of staking formula.

The plan works like this. Choose one horse each day of the racing week. Selections should be based on sound form principles but the deciding factor in arriving at a final choice is the probable starting price. On Monday and Tuesday look for a 2–1 shot. For the next two days aim to find winners around 4–1. Bets for Friday and Saturday are chosen from horses priced at about 6–1. The price requirements for particular days apply irrespective of the number of winners and losers backed.

Stakes are regulated in the following way:

Monday	2–1	3 pts
Tuesday	2–1	3 pts
Wednesday	4–1	1½ pts
Thursday	4–1	1½ pts
Friday	6–1	1 pt
Saturday	6–1	1 pt

Now one might well ask: why not begin by trying to pick at winner at 6–1? The answer is quite simply that it is easier to find one at 2–1. Obviously it is desirable to win as early in the week as possible. In the event of failure one is faced with the choice of increasing stakes or selecting a better-priced winner. The pitfalls inherent in rising stake progressions have already been outlined. It must be far safer in the long term to try for winners at better prices. Now if things can be so arranged mathematically that stakes can actually be reduced without sacrificing the chance of a profit, then so much the better. This is exactly what the COUNTERPOISE method does.

Beginning with a 6–1 selection, one might as well try to find one every day. Rather this plan aims at finding easy winners first so that there is cash in hand for later bets on horses at longer odds. The mathematics of the formula are such that one is quite justified in reducing stakes as the week advances, whether one has won or lost earlier in the week. More gains are wanted after a win but not at the risk of dissipating existing profits. Because it reduces stakes on longer-priced selections, the formula achieves this double objective. On the other hand an early loss means that one is looking to limit losses. Again the plan does the trick – stakes are diminishing and yet a winner or winners at good prices could still pull the fat out of the fire.

A mathematical arrangement of prices and stakes, however sound, cannot produce profits out of thin air. Winners still have to be backed. Given the ability to find some winners, the mathematics of the plan enable calculations to be made in advance as to how much can be won or lost. With just one winner from six bets the maximum loss on the week will be 4 points and possibly less. Two winners, a reasonable expectation for the average competent backer, will provide an overall gain of between 3 and 7 points, depending on which horses actually win. Three winners guarantee a profit of at least 10½ points and possibly a good deal more. Four or more winners must yield a handsome return.

The one problem is being dependent on a betting forecast for the purpose of determining the daily selections. Fluctuations inevitably arise from market operations on the racecourse, so that betting-forecast predictions seldom correspond exactly to actual returned starting prices. In fact this is not too serious a drawback. One may just as well gain as lose from this and in the long run things should even themselves out. The basic soundness of the formula will do the rest.

Finally it is necessary to say a word about methods of selection. Since the largest stakes go on to the 2–1 chances, special care must be exercised in choosing them. Here the search is for out-and-out form horses but at the same time avoiding the apparent good things which will start at really short prices close to odds-on. For the 4–1 selections it is necessary to concentrate on second favourites with sound form in small fields where the favourite is quoted at upwards of 2–1 and so is not greatly fancied. The best way of singling out a 6–1 shot worth backing is to make a list of all horses in the right price category. Examine each in the light of recent form; winning or good placed form in similar company as revealed by a comparison of race values or grade will lead to some live candidates.

So the COUNTERPOISE method offers backers plenty of scope for making their own judgements. It is rigid in terms of selections being governed by the likely starting price but it is possible that a lot of backers who frequently find themselves spoilt for choice on a busy day's racing may well benefit from this discipline.

A mathematical plan is not an automatic road to racing riches but faulty staking is probably the biggest single reason why most backers lose. A reasonable aptitude for picking winners means the COUNTERPOISE method will help to maximise successes.

49
THE 19 WAYS TO WIN DOUBLES FORMULA

A lot of backers achieve consistent results without ever managing to turn them into overall profit. They follow racing closely, know the form book well and can pick out two or three sound wagers each day that are certain to go close at decent prices. Yet in the long run they lose – too many near misses, good seconds and thirds eat into the gains from winners. If the readers falls into this category of punter then the 19 WAYS TO WIN formula is one to consider.

The trick is to link up one horse from one race with two from another in singles and each-way doubles. Suppose you select Horse A as a banker for the first race and decide on Horse B and Horse C for the second leg. The full bet is written as follows:

Race 1	Race 2
1 pt win A	½ pt win B
	½ pt win C

1 pt each-way double A and B
1 pt each-way double A and C

For a 6-point stake this series of bets offers no less than 19 chances of a return. The possible combinations are set out in full below.

1 A wins and B wins.   C places
   Result: 2 win singles, 1 win double, 2 place doubles.

2 A wins and C wins.   B places
   Result: 2 win singles, 1 win double, 2 place doubles.

3 A wins and B wins.   C loses
   Result: 2 win singles, 1 win double, 1 place double.

4 A wins and C wins.   B loses
   Result: 2 win singles, 1 win double, 1 place double.

5 A wins and B places.   C places
   Result: 1 win single, 2 place doubles.

6   A wins and B places.   C loses
     Result: 1 win single, 1 place double.

7   A wins and C places.   B loses
     Result: 1 win single, 1 place double.

8   A wins and B loses.   C loses
     Result: 1 win single.

9   B wins and A places.   C places
     Result: 1 win single, 2 place doubles.

10 B wins and A places.   C loses
     Result: 1 win single, 1 place double.

11 B wins and C places.   A loses
     Result: 1 win single.

12 B wins and A loses.   C loses
     Result: 1 win single.

13 C wins and A places.   B places
     Result: 1 win single, 2 place doubles.

14 C wins and A places.   B loses
     Result: 1 win single, 1 place double.

15 C wins and B places.   A loses
     Result: 1 win single.

16 C wins and A loses.   B loses
     Result: 1 win single.

17 A places and B places.   C places
     Result: 2 place doubles.

18 A places and B places.   C loses
     Result: 1 place double.

19 A places and C places.   B loses
    Result: 1 place double.

Each-way doubles are definitely value bets for the careful punter. The 19 WAYS TO WIN system with its clever combination of win singles and each-way doubles on three horses has tremendous scope. Many of the winning permutations will produce a really good gain on the day. Other patterns of results will recover some or all of the stake. Thus there is plenty of insurance against those all-too-frequent near misses that usually mean total failure. There are even two chances of finding the winner in one race with very little wastage of stakes.

Since place betting at fractions of win odds is involved, a lot depends on prices. Clearly short-priced favourites should be avoided and whilst the banker should be an obvious form horse at fair odds, it is often worth taking a chance with a selection at a really good price as a danger to the first choice in the second leg. In the hands of a skilled punter who knows the form and can pick out value-for-money wagers in the right races, this staking formula is in a class of its own.

50
THE WEEKENDER

For the most part the treble chance mentality is absent among followers of horse racing. Few punters seriously expect to make a fortune, even a small one, from the sport. In fact the majority do not try. By and large they look for small regular gains from their betting while hoping for an occasional nice touch measured in tens, not thousands, of pounds to make the whole thing worthwhile.

Yet there is absolutely no reason why multiple cumulative wagers should not be used to aim for a jackpot payout. If these can be arranged so that the prospect of smaller wins on a regular basis is retained, then such a bet must represent a really attractive proposition. The WEEKENDER goes a long way towards achieving this dual aim.

Saturday always sees a lot of racing up and down the country with plenty of opportunities to sort out an above-average number of good bets. The WEEKENDER requires six selections. Since the system is made up of doubles, trebles and accumulators, it is not necessary to have a series of rank outsiders to produce the big win that is its ultimate goal. A judicious mixture of well-backed form horses with one or two at longer prices will do very nicely. This should not be too much of a problem. There are lots of ways of finding winners at all kinds of odds outlined in this volume.

Having chosen six horses in different races, number them 1 to 6 as in the example below. The system depends on a set of firm guarantees, so this order, once decided upon, must be adhered to throughout when writing the full bet.

1 Chesterfield
2 No Tricks
3 Gala Day
4 Extra Strain
5 Marcus Superbus
6 Directory

The sequence of doubles, trebles and accumulators which makes up the WEEKENDER is as follows:

Doubles
    1 and 3   1 and 6   2 and 4   2 and 5   3 and 6   4 and 5
Trebles
          1, 2 and 5   1, 3 and 5   1, 4 and 6
          2, 3 and 4   2, 3 and 6   4, 5 and 6
Accumulators
          1, 2, 3 and 4   1, 2, 5 and 6
          3, 4, 5 and 6   1, 2, 3, 4, 5 and 6

So in our example the whole bet would be:

Doubles	Trebles	Accumulators
Chesterfield	Chesterfield	Chesterfield
Gala Day	No Tricks	No Tricks
————	Marcus Superbus	Gala Day
Chesterfield	————	Extra Strain
Directory	Chesterfield	————
————	Gala Day	Chesterfield
No Tricks	Marcus Superbus	No Tricks
Extra Strain	————	Marcus Superbus
————	Chesterfield	Directory
No Tricks	Extra Strain	————
Marcus Superbus	Directory	Gala Day
————	————	Extra Strain
Gala Day	No Tricks	Marcus Superbus
Directory	Gala Day	Directory
————	Extra Strain	————
Extra Strain	————	Chesterfield
Marcus Superbus	No Tricks	No Tricks
————	Gala Day	Gala Day
	Directory	Extra Strain
	————	Marcus Superbus
	Extra Strain	Directory
	Marcus Superbus	————
	Directory	
	————	

Each group of wagers has a definite guarantee. Two winners may produce a winning double; three guarantee it. Similarly a treble is certain with four winners and a possibility with only three. Five successes mean you must land a four-horse accumulator, although only four can do the trick. Multiple winners, therefore, can add up to an impressive array of doubles, trebles and four-timers and, if all the selections win, every one of the 16 separate bets, including the six-timer, must score.

In other words, the WEEKENDER method is a balanced wager that can be used for a weekly tilt at a gigantic payout without sacrificing the possibility of regular small-scale profits. For the small backer there is every prospect of plenty of bread and butter. There might be quite a wait for the honey, but the chance of it is always there.

PART 3

Making a 'Backer's Book'

How to beat the bookmakers at their own game

Introduction

Most people who know something about racing are aware that bookmakers bet to figures even if they may be rather vague about the precise *modus operandi*. They could also be perhaps more than just a bit hazy about the mathematics of odds and chances in their own betting. Yet a common dream among racing folk of all sorts is that they might be able to counteract the layers' advantage by some figure system of their own if only they had the necessary mathematical expertise.

Is it ever possible to beat the 'book' by mathematical means? The answer is a definite 'no' if mathematics alone are used, for the edge built into the odds offered by any competent racecourse bookmaker can never be completely eroded, no matter how the backer juggles with stakes. The same applies to the odds received from a race meeting via satellite into betting shops, as well as the final starting price returns formulated by independent Press representatives working in the Ring. The truth is that the bookmakers' method is just about foolproof, certainly over a reasonable period of time and at least in dealing with the totality of punters who bet with one bookmaking firm or another.

Nevertheless, the individual backer can also adopt a mathematical approach to enhance the prospect of a credit balance, both on single races and on a lot of races spread over several days, weeks or even months. Provided sound methods of selection are employed that regularly throw up a healthy supply of winners, regulation of stakes in relation to the odds by mathematical prescription can go a long way towards wresting the initiative from the bookmaker.

In fact there is a way by which punters may win through manipulating stakes and odds so as to make a backer's book. This method is an attempt to beat the bookmakers at their own game by using, in a slightly different way, the system that they themselves use.

Before explaining in detail how to go about this, it is necessary to understand how racecourse bookmakers conduct their business, for the prices they show on their boards before each race are much more than a series of educated guesses. Their reading of form comes into it, together with any knowledge they have about the home form of horses but the range of odds in the context of a whole race is in fact calculated by mathematical principles. This ensures that the odds are definitely and decisively to their own advantage and contrary to that of punters. The basis of these calculations and in fact the basis of all professional bookmaking operations is the following table of odds converted to percentage probabilities. Note that the conversions in this table are to one place after the decimal point. This is sufficiently accurate for normal bookmaking requirements and, as we shall see, for backers too.

51
TABLE OF ODDS AND PERCENTAGES

Odds	Percentage probability	Odds	Percentage probability	Odds	Percentage probability
1–5	83.3	5–4	44.4	9–1	10.0
2–9	81.8	11–8	42.1	19–2	9.5
1–4	80.0	6–4	40.0	10–1	9.1
2–7	77.8	13–8	38.1	11–1	8.3
30–100	76.9	7–4	36.4	12–1	7.7
1–3	75.0	15–8	34.8	13–1	7.1
4–11	73.3	2–1	33.3	14–1	6.7
2–5	71.4	85–40	32.0	15–1	6.3
40–95	70.4	9–4	30.8	16–1	5.9
4–9	69.2	95–40	29.6	18–1	5.3
40–85	68.0	5–2	28.6	20–1	4.8
1–2	66.7	11–4	26.7	22–1	4.3
8–15	65.2	3–1	25.0	25–1	3.8
4–7	63.6	100–30	23.1	28–1	3.4
8–13	61.9	7–2	22.2	30–1	3.2
4–6	60.0	4–1	20.0	33–1	2.9
8–11	57.9	9–2	18.2	35–1	2.8
4–5	55.6	5–1	16.7	40–1	2.4
5–6	54.5	11–2	15.4	50–1	2.0
10–11	52.4	6–1	14.3	66–1	1.5
20–21	51.2	13–2	13.3	100–1	1.0
Evens	50.0	7–1	12.5	150–1	0.7
21–20	48.8	15–2	11.8	200–1	0.5
11–10	47.6	8–1	11.1	250–1	0.4
6–5	45.5	17–2	10.5	500–1	0.2

At first sight all this may look unfathomable but it is really very simple. A look at the table gives the obvious example that a horse quoted at evens can be said to have a 50 per cent chance of winning. Two horses both priced at evens add up to a probability of 100 per cent and would make a 'round' book in a two-horse race. Again, the probability for a 6–4 shot is 40 per cent, whereas 4–1 represents a 20 per cent chance. One horse at the former and three at the latter would also constitute a perfectly 'round' book of 100 per cent in a four-horse contest.

52
Bookmaking

A knowledge of the percentages in the table are second nature to the bookmakers, for their livings depend on it. In the hectic few minutes before the start of a race, as money flows in from the punters, each layer may not worry greatly about the fractions, but each one knows that the percentages for the odds offered about all the runners must together remain above an aggregate of 100 to give a viable trading margin. When this is the case, and it nearly always is, except on those rare occasions when some bookmakers are prepared to bet a point or two below 100 to attract business in a highly competitive market, the book is said to be 'over-round'.

In the unlikely event of the aggregated percentages for the prices on a race in any one book dropping below 100, the layer is betting 'under-round' or 'over-broke'. In this case, or more likely by taking the best of the prices from several competing bookmakers, the alert backer could, by simply staking the percentage of the odds obtainable about each runner converted to pounds, or sums in exact proportion, back every horse in the race and be sure of a profit.

However, most of the time backers must face an 'over-round' book. Here is an example drawn from the starting price returns on a recent 2000 Guineas at Newmarket:

2000 GUINEAS STAKES. NEWMARKET. 1M.

		Odds converted to probability	True odds	True probability of winning
7–2	ORPEN	22.2%	15–1	6.3%
7–1	ENRIQUE	12.5%	15–1	6.3%
15–2	AUCTION HOUSE	11.8%	15–1	6.3%
8–1	COMMANDER COLLINS	11.1%	15–1	6.3%
9–1	MUJAHID	10.0%	15–1	6.3%
10–1	ISLAND SANDS	9.1%	15–1	6.3%
10–1	COMPTON ADMIRAL	9.1%	15–1	6.3%
14–1	ALRASSAAM	6.7%	15–1	6.3%
20–1	BAHAMIAN BANDIT	4.8%	15–1	6.3%
20–1	EXEAT	4.8%	15–1	6.3%
20–1	BRANCASTER	4.8%	15–1	6.3%
25–1	EASAAR	3.8%	15–1	6.3%
33–1	RED SEA	2.9%	15–1	6.3%
50–1	DESARU	2.0%	15–1	6.3%
66–1	GOLD ACADEMY	1.5%	15–1	6.3%
66–1	DEBBIE'S WARNING	1.5%	15–1	6.3%
		118.6%		100.8%

Thus the over-round here is 18.6 per cent. Therefore in the theoretical event of one bookmaker's clients staking according to the percentages, they will stake 118.6 units, but whatever horse wins the bookmaker must return only 100.8 units (the 0.8 per cent difference from 100 per cent is due to the rounding up of the true probability to 6.3 per cent, representing true odds of 15–1 in a 16-horse field). This produces a theoretical profit on the race for the bookmaker of:

$$\frac{18.6}{118.6} \times 100 = 15.7 \text{ per cent}$$

Thus, if a total of £1,186 is bet in line with the percentages, £125 would go on say, Enrique which would cost the bookmaker a payout of £125 × 7 + £125 stake = £1,000 and produce a gain of £186 had it won. If £91 is invested on the actual winner of the race,

Island Sands at 10–1, the bookmaker again returns £1,000 (actually £1,001 due to the rounding up of the probability percentage) and keeps £186. In this way there is always that amount of profit for the layer whatever the result of the race.

This in essence is the system of the racecourse bookmaker and that is why, in theory, the bookmaker should win. In reality it is a practical impossibility that a group of clients patronising one firm will actually bet so conveniently for both the bookmaker and the theory.

To understand why the theory still works out well in practice for the bookmaker in most real cases, an examination of the following table shows the advantage or otherwise to the layer when the probability percentages for the odds on offer are compared with the true mathematical probability of each horse winning.

2000 Guineas Stakes. Newmarket. 1m.

	Odds converted to probability	True probability	Bookmaker's advantage	Backer's advantage
7–2 ORPEN	22.2%	6.3%	15.9%	
7–1 ENRIQUE	12.5%	6.3%	6.2%	
15–2 AUCTION HOUSE	11.8%	6.3%	5.5%	
8–1 COMMANDER COLLINS	11.1%	6.3%	4.8%	
9–1 MUJAHID	10.0%	6.3%	3.7%	
10–1 ISLAND SANDS	9.1%	6.3%	2.8%	
10–1 COMPTON ADMIRAL	9.1%	6.3%	2.8%	
14–1 ALRASSAAM	6.7%	6.3%	0.4%	
20–1 BAHAMIAN BANDIT	4.8%	6.3%		1.5%
20–1 EXEAT	4.8%	6.3%		1.5%
20–1 BRANCASTER	4.8%	6.3%		1.5%
25–1 EASAAR	3.8%	6.3%		2.5%
33–1 RED SEA	2.9%	6.3%		3.4%
50–1 DESARU	2.0%	6.3%		4.3%
66–1 GOLD ACADEMY	1.5%	6.3%		4.8%
66–1 DEBBIE'S WARNING	1.5%	6.3%		4.8%
	118.6%	100.8%	42.1%	24.3%
	–100.8%		–24.3%	
	–17.8%		–17.8%	

The reason why the bookmaker wins in the end should now be obvious. In this example, for the first eight horses in the race, that is all the really fancied horses and the only ones that have a realistic chance on form, the layer offers below the true odds in every single case. Every horse with real potential is running for the 'book' and against the backer, who is left with only a series of small advantages for the 'rags' of the race.

It is simply not true, however, that the bookmakers cannot lose. If most of the money on a race is for the favourite, as it usually is, they will lose on that race when the favourite wins. The only defence if it is considered a 'good thing' is to shorten it up and lengthen the odds about the remainder of the runners in the hope of diverting cash away from the 'jolly'. That way the layers can reduce their liabilities about the favourite, but there are times when they must pay up, hopefully with a smile. On the other hand the fact that beaten favourites outnumber winning favourites in the ratio of about 65 to 35 means that on a typical day most bookmakers win on balance and go home with a sound profit for their endeavours.

53
THE 'BACKER'S BOOK'

How does this short course on bookmaking help the backer? The answer is that the backer can learn much from the bookmaker, for whilst bookmakers are never guilty of constructing a 'book' in a way that leaves them vulnerable over time, punters by contrast frequently fall prey to faulty staking in their attempts to relieve the layers of their money.

EXAMPLE I

A recent race for the November Handicap appeared to be between four candidates, one of which could easily have won. The horses selected might have been Hieroglyphic at 11–4, Church Missionary at 12–1, together with Comstock and Lift and Load, both priced at 20–1. This gave four chances to win, and has already reduced the bookmaker's favourable position to some extent. But to press home the potential advantage stakes must be placed correctly. This is where most punters' problems begin. Let us assume that bets of £10 on each horse are placed in the local betting shop, taking the prices available just before the 'off'. The resulting wager is a completely unbalanced series of bets.

Bet	Odds	Horse	Return on win	Gain/loss on total outlay
£10	11–4	HIEROGLYPHIC	£37.50	−£2.50
£10	12–1	CHURCH MISSIONARY	£130.00	+£90.00
£10	20–1	COMSTOCK	£210.00	+£170.00
£10	20–1	LIFT AND LOAD	£210.00	+£170.00

£40 outlay

There is a wide discrepancy between the potential profit from a victory for Church Missionary when compared with the possible gain from the two outsiders but, if Hieroglyphic wins, as was the case, there is actually a small loss on the race. Despite finding the winner, a stake of £40 returned only £37.50 before tax. Regularly confronted with this sort of bet from clients, the bookmakers are laughing all the way to the bank.

Far better on this set of horses and prices to adjust stakes using the table of odds and percentages, thus acting like a bookmaker in reverse:

Total stake £40 on horses at 11–4 (26.7%), 12–1 (7.7%), 20–1 (4.8%), 20–1 (4.8%).
Backer's percentage of the 'book': 44 per cent.

Stakes on each horse (to the nearest 5p or 10p):

HEIROGLYPHIC $\qquad$ £40 $\times \dfrac{26.7}{44}$ at 11–4 = £24.30

CHURCH MISSIONARY $\qquad$ £40 $\times \dfrac{7.7}{44}$ at 12–1 = £ 7.00

COMSTOCK $\qquad$ £40 $\times \dfrac{4.8}{44}$ at 20–1 = £ 4.35

LIFT AND LOAD $\qquad$ £40 $\times \dfrac{4.8}{44}$ at 20–1 = £ 4.35

Bet	Odds	Horse	Return on win
£24.30	11–4	HIEROGLYPHIC	£91.13
£ 7.00	12–1	CHURCH MISSIONARY	£91.00
£ 4.35	20–1	COMSTOCK	£91.35
£ 4.35	20–1	LIFT AND LOAD	£91.35

Outlay £40.00

Pre-tax profit if any horse wins: £51.00 (to the nearest £).

Now the advantage of making a 'backer's book' becomes apparent. In this second wager Hieroglyphic is a winner in the 'book', not a loser as previously. The punter has taken 44 per cent of the chances in the race, leaving the bookmaker with 56 per cent but the margin is not 44 per cent. It is in fact £^{5}⁄$_{40}$ $\times$ 100 = 127.5 per cent. This surely is a very acceptable profit. It is not possible to have nearly every horse in the race on the backer's side, in the same way that the bookmaker, accepting a large liability on the favourite, contrives to have the whole field without the favourite running for a conventional layer's 'book'. Nevertheless by adjusting stakes to the odds in a similar manner to the bookmakers adjusting their odds to the stakes bet by their clients, a punter can have a significant number of horses in a race and still retain the prospect of a worthwhile win.

54
OPPOSING WEAK FAVOURITES

This method of 'making a book against the book' need not be confined to just handicaps where better prices are usually on offer. It can also be worked successfully on non-handicaps where the winners will probably come from the fancied horses starting at comparatively short odds.

EXAMPLE I

A recent race for the Nassau Stakes from the Glorious Goodwood meeting showed the following odds:

15–8	ALBORADA
7–2	CAPE VERDI
5–1	ZAHRAT DUBAI
7–1	KISSOGRAM
9–1	LADY IN WAITING
10–1	ALABAQ
16–1	JUVENIA
50–1	DIAMOND WHITE

Suppose that the race is thought to be between Alborada, Zahrat Dubai and Alabaq. As we have seen, a level stake on each horse would be a completely unbalanced wager. From an equal division of the stake the punter gains least from the shortest priced horses. Yet these are precisely the selections likely to win most often over a period of time.

The following wager is therefore hopeless:

Bet	Odds	Horse	Pre-tax gain/loss on total outlay
£10	15–8	ALBORADA	−£1.25
£10	5–1	ZAHRAT DUBAI	+£30.00
£10	10–1	ALABAQ	+£80.00

Outlay £30

In this wager again Alborada would have actually lost money if it had won, and Zahrat Dubai would have produced a profit of only £30 compared with the £80 due from the outsider. It is far better to make a backer's book in the recommended manner.

To get away from an aggregated £10 per horse in our examples, this time £50 is spread among bets on the three selected runners.

Total stake £50 on horses at 15–8 (34.8%), 5–1 (16.7%), 10–1 (9.1%).
Backer's percentage of the 'book': 60.6 per cent.

The stake on each horse would be:

ALBORADA $\qquad$ £50 $\times \dfrac{34.8}{60.6}$ at 15–8 = £28.70

ZAHRAT DUBAI $\qquad$ £50 $\times \dfrac{16.7}{60.6}$ at 5–1 = £13.80

ALABAQ $\qquad$ £50 $\times \dfrac{9.1}{60.6}$ at 10–1 = £ 7.50

Betting on three horses led to the following situation:

Bet	Odds	Horse	Return on win
£28.70	15–8	ALBORADA	£82.51
£13.80	5–1	ZAHRAT DUBAI	£82.80
£ 7.50	10–1	ALABAQ	£82.50

Outlay £50.00

Pre-tax profit if any horse wins: £32.50 (to the nearest 50p).

The backer is betting here at approximately 5–3 on, odds which would suit a professional punter, but probably not someone betting in small sums.

However, let us look at the race again. The favourite, Alborada had won the Champion Stakes at Newmarket the previous autumn and had shown herself to be a top-class filly by defeating some of the best 10-furlong horses in the land. The race under consideration was run at the big August meeting at Goodwood nearly 10 months later. Alborada had been off the course since her Newmarket victory. Up against some high-class fillies in this Nassau Stakes there was always the distinct possibility that, lacking a racecourse outing, she might not be able to do herself justice because she was not at her peak. And so, in the event, it proved.

The shrewd punter might easily have made the correct assumption about Alborada and modified the original bet on the race to make this attractive wager:

Total stake £50 on two horses at 5–1 (16.7%), 10–1 (9.1%).
Backer's percentage of the 'book': 25.8 per cent.

The stake on each horse would be:

ZAHRAT DUBAI $£50 \times \dfrac{16.7}{25.8}$ at 5–1 = £32.35

ALABAQ $£50 \times \dfrac{9.1}{25.8}$ at 10–1 = £17.65

Betting on two horses led to the following situation:

Bet	Odds	Horse	Return on win
£32.35	5–1	ZAHRAT DUBAI	£194.10
£17.65	10–1	ALABAQ	£194.15

Outlay £50.00

Pre-tax profit if any horse wins: £144.10 (to the nearest 5p).

Now the backer has a bet at nearly 3–1 for the two horses coupled against the favourite, and it is not necessary to bet in large amounts to achieve a worthwhile return from such wagers.

Conclusion: In fact it is in betting against weak favourites that some modern professionals make the most effective use of the backer's book. Despite vastly improved press coverage of the sport in the present era, there are still enough false favourites in racing to make this a paying strategy. Not even every horse starting at odds-on has a genuinely odds-on chance. An intimate knowledge of the form book will reveal to the trained eye lots of examples of races in which the bookmakers ask for odds about a favourite which in reality may very well not win.

In weak betting markets at small meetings this is a regular occurrence. The backer who can knock out an odds-on favourite and find the winner of the race from two or three opponents in a small field, adjusting stakes in the manner recommended, is very close to being a bookmaker. Both the bookmaker and the professional backer want the 'jolly' beaten for the same reason. Selectivity is essential for the latter who must choose races in which to bet with the utmost care, but given the necessary skill, winning becomes nothing more than a matter of technique.

EXAMPLE 2

A 2m 1f novice hurdle event run at Newton Abbot on Wednesday, 2 August in the year in which I write.

There were just four runners in the race. Lord Rochester was an uneasy favourite, going from 7–4 on to evens in the pre-race betting exchanges before lodging at 11–10 on at the 'off'. Second best in the market was Lenango, heavily backed at evens. Hope Value was a solid 7–1 chance, whilst the 'rag', Ghaazi, was available at 20–1.

Lord Rochester's drift in the market was a clear signal that he was no certainty, although this would not have been decisive without sound reasons to account for it. However, there were aspects of Lord Rochester's form which gave cause for alarm.

He had won twice and been second in three Class E novice hurdles in May before being rested in June. When he reappeared in July, in his most recent run, he was raised one grade to Class D, but could only finish third, 3½ lengths and 1¾ lengths behind the easy winner, Gimmick. The form book noted ominously that he had been 'soon beaten' after the second-last hurdle. Clearly, despite the lay-off, the jump in class had caused the horse to struggle and, although his opponents were relatively inexperienced, today's race was still officially graded 'D' also. In addition, Lord Rochester was required to give them 11 lb or 12 lb as a penalty for his earlier victories in the weaker grade.

To a seasoned observer things would have been looking bad for Lord Rochester, but surely the final straw was the fact that for the first time in his career over hurdles he was not to be ridden by an experienced professional jockey, but by a five pounds claimer who was in the saddle presumably to alleviate the worst effects of the penalty he had to carry.

Thus connections had betrayed a clear lack of confidence in the horse's chance, and as we have seen, there was no confidence behind him in the Ring either.

Of his opponents, Lenango had run on to be fourth of 11 in a Class D race last time out, his first appearance over hurdles. Hope Value had similarly made his hurdling debut last time, when he had been noted as a 'bit backward', but ran quite well to be sixth of 13 over today's course and distance, again in a Class D event. Thus both horses were entitled to improve quite a bit. Ghaazi, the outsider, had never run before.

This was a classic case of a weak favourite which, though starting at a shade of odds-on, looked ripe for defeat. The shrewd punter could have entered the betting in the following manner:

Total stake £50 on two horses, one at evens (50%) and one at 7–1 (12.5%).
Backer's percentage of the 'book': 62.5 per cent.

Stakes on each horse:

LENANGO $£50 \times \dfrac{50}{62.5}$ at evens = £40

HOPE VALUE $£50 \times \dfrac{12.5}{62.5}$ at 7–1 = £10

Betting on just two horses had the following result:

Bet	Odds	Horse	Return on win
£40.00	evens	LENANGO	£80.00
£10.00	7–1	HOPE VALUE	£80.00

Outlay £50.00

Pre-tax profit if any horse wins: £30.

For realising that Lord Rochester was highly unlikely to win, the backer could have won £3 for every £5 staked, this time in a very small field of moderate horses.

In the actual race Lord Rochester again weakened two hurdles from home to be beaten into second place, no less than 19 lengths behind the winner, Hope Value, with Lenango 1¼ lengths away third.

Conclusion: Races like this do not occur every day, but there are still plenty of them over a season, particularly in jump races. You can always make a mistake and see the favourite romp home with the horses you have backed trailing in its wake, but the clever punter with an expert knowledge of the form book and the ability to read the signs correctly should get it right most of the time. There are no certainties in racing form, but surely the sport offers no more straightforward way of making money than the above race and others like it.

55
BIG HANDICAPS

There is one other kind of race in which skilled operators can win consistently by making their own 'book'. This method too is by no means infallible, but a little flair in working the bet can land some really nice coups.

At regular intervals throughout the Flat season bookmakers are happy to offer ante-post prices for big handicaps. There are also a number of races of this kind during the National Hunt season, beginning with the Thomas Pink Gold Cup at Cheltenham in November.

The trick in taking a good profit from these races is to time one's bets correctly, for the market on a big handicap generally goes through a number of stages.

When the prices from the layers first appear, some time before the race, betting is a lottery. Final running plans are not known, and only someone genuinely 'in the know' can avoid backing non-runners.

After the five-day declaration stage a much clearer picture emerges and a realistic set of prices becomes available. At this point the backer should go carefully through all the form and make a note of all those horses which have a sound chance of winning. This group should be rather larger than the intended final bet to be struck when the backer has arrived at definite conclusions about prospects. The draw and the way the bookmakers price up the race just after the overnight declaration is known will quite possibly cause some modification of original ideas.

Eve-of-race bets are not ante-post, but on a 'non-runner, no bet' basis. It is at this point that a final list of candidates for the big race should be settled on and all bets struck. Do not wait until the next day. That will be the morning of the race and whatever value is left from the overnight prices framed at about midday on the previous day will go in the betting exchanges once the bookmakers start taking bets from the 'early birds'. There is no need to worry, however. Backers' bets are 'on' immediately after the 'overnight' when in possession of all the facts such as the draw and non-runners. The prices obtained are fixed.

The final stage in the market is betting on the course in the time leading up to the 'off'. Here again there may be another shrinkage in value for the odds about a few horses as the bookmakers assess their final liabilities. But again this does not affect bets already laid. Value has already been obtained and, if a horse does not come under starting orders for any reason, your money is returned.

Exceptional value from the very best of the odds requires bets to be made immediately after the five-day declaration is announced. Most connections will not have paid the final forfeit if they do not really intend to run their horse, so the small gamble of backing an occasional non-runner is more than offset by the opportunity to obtain much better prices. Horses to avoid are those with a light weight which may not get into the race if all the higher-weighted horses stand their ground. These can always be backed later if and when their participation becomes certain. Also, if the draw is likely to have a big effect on the race, it is wise to wait for the overnight declaration before making a commitment. These considerations apart, a wager struck just after the five-day stage will provide some very 'tasty' prices about many horses whose odds will gradually shrink.

EXAMPLE I

A recent running of the Lincoln Handicap over one mile at Doncaster will highlight most of the important points about making a backer's book in big handicaps.

In the figure following the prices on offer from one big bookmaking firm at about midday on the eve of the race are shown on the left, that is shortly after the overnight declaration and the draw for the race were announced. On the right are the actual starting prices. Since even the biggest handicap usually goes to a fancied candidate these days, only prices for the first 12 horses in the betting are given. Unless there are special grounds for including an extreme outsider, a list of this length will nearly always include the winner, and it is in this area that bets should be concentrated.

LINCOLN HANDICAP. DONCASTER. 1M.

Horse	Pre-race odds	Starting price	Draw
TAYSEER	9–2	8–1	6
JOHN FERNELEY	8–1	7–1	1
RIGHT WING	10–1	9–1	21
MUCHEA	14–1	12–1	7
RIVER TIMES	16–1	12–1	4
PANTAR	20–1	16–1	8
ZANAY	20–1	14–1	10
ROCK FALCON	20–1	25–1	12
NAVIASKY	20–1	16–1	20
THE WHISTLING TEAL	20–1	7–1	18
KING PRIAM	25–1	25–1	2
SILK ST JOHN	25–1	25–1	17

Only two horses had remained at the same odds, two had drifted in price, but no less than eight of the first dozen in the betting had shortened up, some of them quite considerably.

Therefore, a bet made immediately after the overnight declaration is likely to beat the final market on the race, not just in this Lincoln Handicap but, in most big races of a similar type. This fact can be the source of excellent profits for backers intent on making their own 'book' on these events.

Note that the above illustration also shows the draw for the Lincoln in question, a factor that year after year has a big influence on the first important betting race of the new Flat season. Reference to the Racecourse Guide in Part 4 reveals that on the straight mile at Doncaster a low draw is favoured in big fields if the ground is soft (or worse). This was exactly the condition of the ground on Town Moor for the renewal of the Lincoln that we have been considering. Low numbers were expected to dominate by those who study statistics, and so it proved.

Following previous examples, assume a 'book' is made around the first five low-drawn horses in the betting. The bets would have been as follows:

Horse	Odds	Percentage
TAYSEER	9–2	18.2%
JOHN FERNELEY	8–1	11.1%
MUCHEA	14–1	6.7%
RIVER TIMES	16–1	5.9%
PANTAR	20–1	4.8%

Backer's percentage of the 'book':   46.7%

Stake on the race: £50.

Bets on each horse:

Calculation	Horse	Odds	Stake	Win returns
$£50 \times \dfrac{18.2}{46.7}$	TAYSEER	9–2	£19.50	£107.25
$£50 \times \dfrac{11.1}{46.7}$	JOHN FERNELEY	8–1	£11.90	£107.10
$£50 \times \dfrac{6.7}{46.7}$	MUCHEA	14–1	£ 7.20	£108.00
$£50 \times \dfrac{5.9}{46.7}$	RIVER TIMES	16–1	£ 6.30	£107.10
$£50 \times \dfrac{4.8}{46.7}$	PANTAR	20–1	£ 5.10	£107.10
			£50.00	

Profit if any of the five win: £57 (approx).

Thus backing the winner makes a profit of around £57, having enjoyed the luxury of staking on no less than five horses in the race for the same profit. Admittedly this particular wager got the wrong end of the odds about the deposed favourite, Tayseer, and only a point was made on the winner, John Ferneley by betting early. But, in many other races the odds might reasonably be more above the starting price for a winning selection. Every time the odds are beaten, profitability is enhanced. Also, in races such as the Royal Hunt Cup, the Cambridgeshire, and a number of others, betting can start at 10–1 the field. The percentage of the 'book' needed to back four, five or even six horses will be reduced where the odds on the whole are proportionately longer, again leading to enhanced profitability from a winning selection.

Conclusion: No matter how many horses in a race are backed, the winner still has to be found and there will be times when it will escape even the widest net made possible by making a backer's book. Nevertheless, even the greatest pessimist would probably agree that betting in the way recommended in the preceding pages, makes life easier in the hazardous business of backing horses. Over a period of time judicious use of a backer's 'book' ought to result in a winning betting ledger.

PART 4

Racecourse Guide

A track-by-track guide to the most significant
betting trends at all courses in Britain

Flat

Ascot

Right-handed. A 1m 6f galloping, triangular course with a stiff 2½f uphill run-in. There is a straight mile with slight undulations.

Grade: A

Effect of the draw: Preconceived notions of the draw's influence under various conditions have taken a knock in recent years. At present the one sound rule is that on the straight track, runners drawn close to either rail are favoured, though where the pace is could decide which side emerges best at the business end of a race. However, with the bias tending to veer from side to side in recent years on the same type of going, the backer's best option is to study early races with big fields at individual meetings, to discover any advantage that currently prevails. The draw has little influence on the round course.

Success rate of all favourites: 24.6 per cent.

Favourites' success rate in two-year-old stakes: 31.6 per cent.

Most significant form: (1st, 2nd, 3rd, 4th last time out) from Sandown. At the Royal meeting, horses that were first or second last time out at Epsom, Haydock, Newbury or Sandown have an excellent record. The Flat season falls into two unequal halves – before Royal Ascot and after. Do not be mesmerised by Royal Ascot form. It is suspect for the future. In the short term in particular, animals which have had a hard race at Ascot in mid-June may take a long time to recover from their exertions.

Trainer tip: J. Dunlop has the best all-round record, but S. bin Suroor has a distinct edge in stakes races.

AYR

Left-handed. This galloping, oval track is just over 1m 4f in length with a 4f run-in. In addition there is a straight 6f.

Grade: D

      C (Western meeting, September)

Effect of the draw: In large fields over 7f and further, low numbers are favoured. When the ground is really soft the low numbers should also have the best of it on the straight course in races such as the Silver and Ayr Gold Cups at the Western meeting.

Success rates of all favourites: 28.6 per cent.

Favourites' success rate in two-year-old stakes: 34.9 per cent.

Most significant form: (1st, 2nd, 3rd, 4th last time out) from York.

Trainer tip: B. Hills does not send all that many runners north but his raiders must be treated with the utmost respect. He has the best winning percentage at the course of all trainers.

BATH

Left-handed. This is a kidney-shaped, turning course of just over 1m 4f, with an uphill run-in of 4f. Races over the 5f 11yd and 5f 161yd distances are run from a chute. Galloping horses are favoured but form from the course often fails to stand up elsewhere.

Grade: D

Effect of the draw: Low numbers are favoured in races of 1m 5yd, but the bias in their favour in sprints is not as pronounced as is sometimes claimed, except in very big fields.

Success rate of all favourites: 32.9 per cent.

Favourites' success rate in two-year-old stakes: 34.3 per cent.

Most significant form: (1st, 2nd, 3rd, 4th last time out) from Salisbury. Pat Eddery rides this course particularly well.

Trainer tip: Local trainer R. Charlton is to be feared, especially in non-handicaps.

BEVERLEY

Right-handed. At 1m 3f undulating, this oval course has an uphill 2½f run-in. The 5f course is on the climb all the way and is especially severe. The downhill run to the straight on the round course can unbalance some horses. Course specialists should be followed.

Grade: D

Effect of the draw: High numbers are dominant in 5f, 7f 100 yd and 1m 100yd races, one of the strongest biases in the entire country. On really soft or heavy ground, however, this advantage is nullified, and those drawn very low are favoured by the way the course drains up the stands' rail.

Success rate of all favourites: 34 per cent.

Favourites' success in two-year-old stakes: 44.1 per cent.

Most significant form: (1st, 2nd, 3rd, 4th last time out) from Beverley itself.

Trainer tip: This track has been a favourite of L. Cumani for many years. Runners from his Newmarket yard have a first-rate record in stakes races especially.

BRIGHTON

Left-handed. A 1m 4f undulating horseshoe, there is a steep downhill run from half a mile out which lasts for 2f. The actual run-in is 3½f. This sharp track is totally unsuited to galloping types. At summer-holiday meetings the ground can become bone hard, favouring top weights. Course specialists do well but the form is suspect for other courses.

Grade: D

Effect of the draw: Low numbers have some advantage in sprints and races up to 7f 214yd, although high numbers should not be ruled out because of their draw alone. When the ground comes up soft, however, fields usually cross over to race up the stands' rail. This can give those drawn high a decisive edge.

Success rate of all favourites: 33 per cent.

Favourites' success in two-year-old stakes: 37.3 per cent.

Most significant form: (1st, 2nd, 3rd, 4th last time out) from Brighton itself. Brighton is on the southern, summer-holiday circuit and horses running within seven days of a win on a small track often 'go in' again.

Trainer tip: Sir M Prescott's handicappers frequently land a 'touch'.

CARLISLE

Right-handed. A 1m 5f undulating, pear-shaped course with easy turns. Strong, long-striding gallopers are favoured by the long run from the start of the final bend 5f out. The 5f 207yd course starts from a chute. There is a stiff 3½f uphill finish.

Grade: E

Effect of the draw: High numbers are supposed to have an advantage over sprint distances, but it would be wrong to make too much of this. Very soft ground on the other hand definitely favours low numbers over 5–6f. But, since the track is not used for Flat racing beyond the third week in August, very soft conditions are the exception.

Success rate of all favourites: 29.7 per cent.

Favourites' success in two-year-old stakes: 51 per cent.

Most significant form: (1st, 2nd, 3rd, 4th last time out) from northern tracks in two-year-old races over the minimum trip. Because Carlisle is a fundamentally fair but testing track, betting coups on juveniles are often engineered by small, local trainers whose owners like to bet.

Trainer tip: Top northern handler M. Johnston is seldom far away here and may continue to show a good profit from runners in every kind of race.

CATTERICK

Left-handed. This is a sharp, undulating oval course of not much more than 1m 1f with a downhill run into a 3f straight. The track is dog-legged. Quick starters have a big advantage in races up to 7f.

Grade: E

Effect of the draw: On soft ground high numbers are definitely best in races over 5f but, on fast ground, this slight advantage may be reversed in favour of those drawn low. On the round course, over 5f 212yd and 7f, low-drawn horses have a significant edge. A slow start, however, can cancel out any draw advantage in races over a short trip.

Success rate of all favourites: 33.7 per cent.

Favourites' success in two-year-old stakes: 40.7 per cent.

Most significant form: (1st, 2nd, 3rd, 4th last time out) from Catterick itself. Horses which have led all the way to win on this and other northern tracks frequently stage a repeat performance.

Trainer tip: B. Hills is a potent force in weight-for-age and stakes races, but his handicappers do not always run well, despite short prices.

CHEPSTOW

Left-handed. A 2m oval course, it is undulating with two sharp turns and a straight run-in of 5f. The straight mile (1m 14yd) is on an extension to the round course.

Grade: D

Effect of the draw: High numbers used to be regarded as favoured on the straight course but, to all intents and purposes, the draw has no influence on results nowadays.

Success rate of all favourites: 30.2 per cent.

Favourites' success in two-year-old stakes: 38.2 per cent.

Trainer tip: Two-year-olds and three-year-olds trained by Sir M. Stoute are well worth backing in non-handicap races.

CHESTER

Left-handed. This is a very tight, flat, circular course of slightly more than 1m. The track turns all the way which favours handy sorts, though long-striding gallopers can overcome the conformation of the course over long distances, especially on soft ground. Sprints are on the round course. Run-in of barely 2f.

Grade: C
          B (May meeting)

Effect of the draw: Low numbers have a big advantage in races of less than a mile provided the horse starts quickly enough to get a good position. Soft ground makes the bias even greater.

Success rate of all favourites: 34.7 per cent.

Favourites' success in two-year-old stakes: 50.7 per cent.

Most significant form: Form works out badly in handicaps here.

Trainer tip: Sir M. Stoute averages one winner in four at the Roodeye and his handicap record is far superior to that of any other handler.

DONCASTER

Left-handed. This flat, galloping conical-shaped course of some 2m has a long 4½f run-in that can find out a horse just lacking in stamina for the trip. There is also a straight mile but races of 1m are run on the straight extension and also on the round course.

Grade: C

A (St Leger meeting, September)

B (first March and late October meetings)

Effect of the draw: The draw is always an issue for the Spring Mile and Lincoln Handicap when low numbers should dominate if the going is on the soft side. In other ground conditions study early results from the meeting to detect any prevailing bias on the straight track. Low numbers have some advantage on the round course, but only in big fields.

Success rate of all favourites: 29 per cent.

Favourites' success in two-year-old stakes: 42.6 per cent.

Most significant form: (1st, 2nd, 3rd, 4th last time out) from Newmarket. The first 10 home in the Lincoln Handicap should be followed until 30 June with a stop-at-a-win policy, a system which has produced some very fine results down the years. In other years though it can come badly unstuck, usually due to too much clashing among qualifiers competing for the same big prizes. Winners at the big September meeting in the stakes races for two-year-olds are nearly always among the very best of their generation. They should be carefully watched as three-year-olds.

Trainer tip: Doncaster has long been a happy hunting ground for the cream of the Newmarket stables. Godolphin's record in stakes races, either for two-year-olds or older horses is outstanding but S. bin Suroor's occasional tilts at handicaps often go astray. H. Cecil makes a speciality of winning non-handicaps at the St Leger meeting.

EPSOM

Left-handed. A 1½m switchback course shaped like a horseshoe. Straight 5f is downhill for 4f with a sharp rise to the post; it is the fastest sprint strip in the world.

Grade: B

    A (Derby meeting)

Effect of the draw: Low numbers are at an advantage on the round course except on soft ground when the runners tend to tack over to the stands' rail to get the higher, better ground. The traditional advantage to high numbers over 5f is easily nullified by a fast break from the stalls.

Success rate of all favourites: 27.6 per cent.

Favourites' success in two-year-old stakes: 48 per cent.

Most significant form: (1st, 2nd, 3rd, 4th last time out) from Lingfield.

Trainer tip: Middleham trainer M. Johnston often launches a successful raid here.

FOLKESTONE

Right-handed. This is a 1m 3f pear-shaped, undulating course with tight bends and a run-in of 2½f. There is also a straight 6f course. Small, handy horses are favoured.

Grade: E

Effect of the draw: There is a strong bias in favour of high-drawn horses over 5f and 6f on any ground, especially when the field is likely to split into two. Heavy ground tends to magnify the bias. High numbers are also at an advantage on the round course.

Success rate of all favourites: 28.1 per cent.

Favourites' success in two-year-old stakes: 30.6 per cent.

Trainer tip: Sir M. Prescott scores freely but his two-year-olds should be passed over.

Goodwood

Mainly right-handed together with a straight 6f. The very fast 5f section is downhill much of the journey. The right-handed loop for races from from 7f to 1m 6f joins the straight course for a long run-in of 4f. Distance races start the reverse way up the straight and turn left-handed into the loop. This is one of the few top tracks in the country with a bias against galloping horses, due to the tight turns.

Grade: A

Effect of the draw: Over 7f and 1m high numbers do best though in soft ground the jockeys usually prefer to challenge up the stands' rail, thus cancelling out the bias from the stalls. The vital edge that favoured high-drawn horses on the straight course in races such as the Stewards' Cup may have been eradicated by recent alterations to the course. However, in very large fields over 5f–6f a position close to either rail is obviously an advantage.

Success rate of all favourites: 32.5 per cent.

Favourites' success in two-year-old stakes: 45.5 per cent.

Most significant form: (1st, 2nd, 3rd, 4th last time out) from Newmarket, Sandown, York and Goodwood itself. Two-year old form in all races, including nurseries, works out extremely well. When the ground rides very fast at the 'Glorious' meeting following first and second favourites from the top yards in every kind of race can reap a handsome reward. The winner and placed horses from the Stewards' Cup generally pay to follow for the rest of the season. Unlike Royal Ascot, the form at the fashionable July/August meeting can be relied upon in the weeks that follow.

Trainer tip: Honours are usually evenly distributed among the top yards, with the smaller stables hardly featuring. Raiders from the north are less successful here than at other big, southern courses with one or two notable exceptions. P. Cole has the best all-round record, with stable plans geared to winning at the course. His runners in handicaps should be noted, regardless of the odds.

HAMILTON PARK

Right-handed. Straight 6f 5yd course. Races from 1m 65yd up to 1m 5f 9yd start in reverse direction and are run round a pear-shaped loop which rejoins the straight course for a 5f run-in with a stiff uphill finish that dips 3f out. The ground can become bottomless in the dip during spells of wet weather. This unique course is sharp but galloping types are not necessarily inconvenienced.

Grade: E

Effect of the draw: High numbers are much the best in all races up to 1m 65yd. In soft ground or worse, conditions that often prevail, low-drawn horses have virtually no chance in sprints. The racecourse executive has recently announced that the stalls will always be placed on the stands' side except when the ground is heavy. This confirmation of what has been the status quo for some time is unlikely to alter the very strong bias against low-drawn horses on the course.

Success rate of all favourites: 32.7 per cent.

Favourites' success in two-year-old stakes: 38.3 per cent.

Most significant form: Despite the low grade of racing here, or perhaps because of it, many runners are sent from the south. Quite a few are beaten at short odds. In fact, a well-known trainer, now sadly deceased, once remarked: 'If you want to get a good horse beaten, take it to Hamilton.'

Trainer tip: M. Channon usually makes the long journey north pay, but his two-year-olds are not to be trusted.

Haydock Park

Left-handed. This is a flat, oval track of 1m 5f with a 4½f run-in which climbs slightly throughout. There is also a straight 6f. The course is a very fair test which favours neither galloping nor handy types.

Grade: B

Effect of the draw: Low numbers do slightly better on the round course in races of 7f 30yd and 1m 30yd but in soft ground most races finish on the stands' side, thus rendering the low-draw advantage ineffective. Recent drainage work may have finally removed the age-old bias towards high numbers in sprints.

Success rate of all favourites: 31.7 per cent.

Favourites' success in two-year-old stakes: 42.6 per cent.

Most significant form: Form from the classier courses is at a premium. Good Haydock winners often go on to better things.

Trainer tip: H. Cecil has a 60 per cent strike rate in two-year-old and weight-for-age races.

KEMPTON PARK

Right-handed. This is a sharp 1m 5f triangular, flat track with a straight course for 5f–6f races which bisects the main circuit. The Jubilee course for 7f up to 1m 2f races joins this at the beginning of the run-in which is about 3½f in length.

Grade: B

Effect of the draw: In races of 5f or 6f low numbers are clearly best in soft ground when the stalls are positioned on the stands' side. When the stalls are on the opposite side of the track, high numbers are best, as they are when a big field is likely to spread right across the course. Fast ground renders the bias much less significant. Although high numbers ought, in theory, to be favoured on the turning 7f and 8f, there is little in the records to support this view.

Success rate of all favourites: 27.7 per cent.

Favourites' success in two-year-old stakes: 27.6 per cent.

Most significant form: (1st, 2nd, 3rd, 4th last time out) from Newmarket.

Trainer tip: R. Charlton has a good record in handicaps.

LEICESTER

Right-handed. A 2m oval course with a run-in of about 5f. Straight course of 1m 8yd, downhill to halfway, then uphill for 2f, finishing on the level.

Grade: C

Effect of the draw: The old bias for low numbers in softish ground on the straight course seems much less important nowadays. In fact, there currently appears to be a faster strip up the centre of the course when overall conditions ride soft. Horses so drawn that they can race there usually seem to benefit.

Success rate of all favourites: 27 per cent.

Favourites' success in two-year-old stakes: 30.8 per cent.

Trainer tip: The elite duo of Sir M. Stoute and H. Cecil dominate the non-handicap races.

LINGFIELD PARK (TURF)

Left-handed. A sharp, triangular course of nearly 1½m with a run-in of 4f, the course rises to the farthest point from the stands then descends into a tight home bend. Horses need to be handy and adaptable. There is a straight 7f 140yd extension to the main circuit which is downhill for most of the way. Course specialists do well and it is regarded as an excellent trial ground for Epsom, being a similar track.

Grade: C

Effect of the draw: The draw has little effect, with neither side of the straight course favoured. The stalls' position has varied in recent years, even for different distances at the same meeting. Until a consistent, settled policy is adopted by the Lingfield authority, the picture is certain to remain confused.

Success rate of all favourites: 33.3 per cent.

Favourites' success in two-year-old stakes: 44.9 per cent.

Trainer tip: The relatively few runners from H. Cecil's yard should always be noted.

LINGFIELD PARK (ALL-WEATHER)

Left-handed. The very sharp equitrack, only 1¼m in circumference, is inside the turf course. There is a short run-in of about 2f. A chute provides a 1m 4f and 1m 5f start.

Grade: E (but form from the equitrack is not reliable on grass)

Effect of the draw: From 5f to 1¼m those drawn in the high stalls are at a considerable disadvantage.

Success rate of all favourites: 31.1 per cent.

Favourites' success in two-year-old stakes: 38.5 per cent.

Trainer tip: No trainer has an outstanding percentage of winners at this competitive venue although D. Chapman's handicappers are seldom there just for the outing.

MUSSELBURGH (EDINBURGH)

Right-handed. A 1m 2f oval track with tight bends and a run-in of 4f together with a straight 5f. Galloping types are at a disadvantage.

Grade: E

Effect of the draw: Over 7f 15yd and 1m 16yd high numbers have the advantage. Low numbers are best over 5f when the stalls are on the stands' side.

Success rate of all favourites: 36.6 per cent.

Favourites' success in two-year-old stakes: 41.3 per cent.

Most significant form: (1st, 2nd, 3rd, 4th last time out) from Newcastle.

Trainer tip: Sir M. Prescott likes a tilt at all kinds of race here. He has a very high strike rate, but it is not always the most fancied animals at short prices that actually succeed.

NEWBURY

Left-handed. This is a 1m 7f oval, galloping track with easy turns and a 5f straight. On the round course races over 7f 64yd and 1m 7yd start from a chute. There is an extension to the main circuit to form a slightly undulating straight mile.

Grade: A

Effect of the draw: When the ground is soft or worse high numbers are heavily favoured, both on the straight and round courses. This even applies in races of up to 1m 5f 61yd.

Success rate of all favourites: 26.1 per cent.

Favourites' success in two-year-old stakes: 38.5 per cent.

Most significant form: (1st, 2nd, 3rd, 4th last time out) from Newmarket.

Trainer tip: J. Gosden is top trainer at the course, his runners showing a level-stakes profit over an extended period. It could well be that his move to Manton, within 20 miles or so of the course, will reinforce and even enhance this trend. Curiously, however, for a handler who places his charges so well, his handicappers performed indifferently when sent from Newmarket.

NEWCASTLE

Left-handed. This is a galloping, triangular circuit of 1m 6f with a stiff uphill 4f run-in. The straight course is 1m 8yd long. The track is exceptionally testing on soft ground.

Grade: C

Effect of the draw: On most ground low numbers have an edge on the straight course. The swing to high numbers being favoured when racing is up the stands' rail now only seems to apply if the going is lightning fast.

Success rate of all favourites: 31.6 per cent.

Favourites' success in two-year-old stakes: 38.9 per cent.

Most significant form: (1st, 2nd, 3rd, 4th last time out) from Beverley for outsiders.

Trainer tip: H. Cecil is the trainer to follow, even in handicaps.

NEWMARKET (ROWLEY MILE COURSE)

Right-handed. Two long straight stretches, beginning at the 2m 2f start out of view of the stands and turn into the exceptionally wide home straight, 10f 'Across the Flat' to an uphill finish from the 'Dip' 1½f out. Galloping types are obviously in their element.

Grade: A

Effect of the draw: There is no bias, although it helps to be racing where the pace is in very big fields.

Success rate of all favourites: 29.5 per cent.

Favourites' success in two-year-old stakes: 39.7 per cent.

Most significant form: As befits the headquarters of racing, Newmarket is very cosmopolitan in terms of the form of competing horses, but Yorkshire stables should be noted for an occasional handicap raid. The booking of a top jockey from the south is often a big clue about an impending coup.

Trainer tip: H. Cecil's three-year-olds should be noted at their home track on their seasonal debut. Do not be put off by long odds – the stable is reputed not to bet.

NEWMARKET (JULY COURSE)

Right-handed. There is a long straight stretch from the 2m 24yd start which turns almost at right angles into the straight Bunbury Mile. The course undulates slightly until it begins to climb to the winning post 1f out. Absolutely fair test which again favours the long-striding animal.

Grade: A

Effect of the draw: None. The course is only used in the summer months when the going is nearly always fast. The rarity of cut in the ground, however, produces no bias.

Success rate of all favourites: 30.4 per cent.

Favourites' success in two-year-old stakes: 41.7 per cent.

Most significant form: (1st, 2nd, 3rd, 4th last time out) from Ascot. Yorkshire trainers specialise in handicap coups on this course as well as on the Rowley Mile.

Trainer tip: L. Cumani often lays out a horse for a handicap from his nearby stable.

NOTTINGHAM

Left-handed. This is a 1m 4f oval course with easy turns and a 4½f straight. There is also a straight 6f 15yd track as an extension to the circuit. The whole arena is exceptionally flat.

Grade: D

Effect of the draw: At Nottingham the stalls are usually placed on the stands' side which gives an edge to high-drawn horses, especially on soft going. When the stalls are occasionally positioned on the far side, low numbers are best, though it would be wrong to make too much of this. Low numbers, however, are definitely at an advantage in big fields on the turning course.

Success rate of all favourites: 30.5 per cent.

Favourites' success in two-year-old stakes: 37.5 per cent.

Trainer tip: Sir M. Prescott has an excellent record in all departments.

PONTEFRACT

Left-handed. A pear-shaped course of about 2m, it is almost all on the turn. The run-in is only 2f long and there is no straight course.

Grade: D

Effect of the draw: Low numbers have a distinct advantage in races up to 1m 4yd. On soft ground, however, the situation changes to the extent that high numbers are then much the best. If, however, the ground is so heavy that the stalls are moved to the outside of the course, the advantage of a high draw is cancelled out. A further factor confusing the picture is that any draw edge will be nullified by a slow start. Nevertheless, the astute punter can make money by mastering the ramifications of the draw at this quirky course.

Success rate of all favourites: 31.4 per cent.

Favourites' success in two-year-old stakes: 47.7 per cent.

Most significant form: Two-year-olds strong enough to win on the stiff sprint course often run well in better company in near-at-hand engagements.

Trainer tip: Not an obvious venue for B. Hills and H. Cecil, but their two-year-olds should be noted, unless running in nursery handicaps.

REDCAR

Left-handed. 1m 5f oval course with a 5f run-in and a straight mile. Though the course is narrow, galloping horses are not inconvenienced.

Grade: C

Effect of the draw: With the draw traditionally supposed to favour high numbers, this is confirmed when the stalls are placed nearest to the stands as they nearly always are. In very big fields, however, quite often a feature of Redcar cards, horses racing out wide in the centre of the course win their share.

Success rate of all favourites: 30.5 per cent.

Favourites' success in two-year-old stakes: 31.7 per cent.

Most significant form: (1st, 2nd, 3rd, 4th last time out) from Thirsk.

Trainer tip: With J. Gosden in new quarters his excellent record has a question mark over it, for his new patrons may have different objectives. J. Dunlop likes to send his juveniles here and they do extremely well in nurseries and stakes races.

RIPON

Right-handed. A 1m 5f undulating, oval circuit, this track has tight bends and a 5f run-in. The straight course is 6f long.

Grade: C

Effect of the draw: There is a slight advantage to high numbers on the round course over a mile. In sprints, although the stalls are usually on the stands' side (low numbers), on fast ground high numbers are much favoured when the field is likely to split into two, enabling them to take a position on the far rail and cash in on a strip of quick ground over there. Low numbers in 5f–6f races seem best in small fields when the entire field races up the stands' rail.

Success rate of all favourites: 31.7 per cent.

Favourites' success in two-year-old stakes: 38.4 per cent.

Trainer tip: M. Channon's two-year-olds merit only a watching brief, but his senior handicappers are well worth an interest. H. Cecil is the man for maidens.

SALISBURY

Right-handed. The straight mile has a dog-leg 5f out and an uphill finish of 4f. Races of more than a mile on a loop which turns sharply right-handed into the straight course for a home run of 6½f. A compact course favouring handier types, though the straight mile suits all horses.

Grade: C

Effect of the draw: Salisbury has a policy of moving the stalls from one side of the track to the other. Also, one type of going does not always produce the same bias. The effect of the draw under a given set of circumstances is therefore difficult to predict, although on very soft ground the low numbers are traditionally favoured on the straight course if the stalls are in the centre or on the stands' sides.

Success rate of all favourites: 33.4 per cent.

Favourites' success in two-year-old stakes: 42.2 per cent.

Most significant form: (1st, 2nd, 3rd, 4th last time out) from Newbury. Two-year-olds often go on to bigger successes at top meetings, making the course Grade B for juveniles.

Trainer tip: The move from Newmarket to Manton should confirm J. Gosden's position as the trainer with the best strike rate and the biggest profit potential.

SANDOWN PARK

Right-handed. A 1m 5f oval course with easy turns but a stiff run-in of just over 4f. The separate 5f course bisecting the main track is also uphill.

Grade: A

Effect of the draw: On the separate 5f course high numbers have a big advantage, particularly when there is a lot of 'give' in the ground and the stalls are on the far side. If the stalls are on the stands' side low numbers are better but only slightly. However, the ground gets progressively faster as the far rail is approached – high numbers may again assert if, in a biggish field, a horse can get across the course without being too far behind the leaders. As the ground gets softer, these trends are magnified proportionately. Over 7f 16yd and 1m 14yd high numbers are marginally superior.

Success rate of all favourites: 29.2 per cent.

Favourites' success in two-year-old stakes: 32.3 per cent.

Trainer tip: Sir M. Stoute leads the non-handicap race division numerically, though S. bin Suroor has an even bigger winning percentage in the same type of race from far less runners.

SOUTHWELL (ALL-WEATHER)

Left-handed. This is quite a sharp, true, oval course with a run-in of about 3f. The fibresand track is outside the grass course. Both courses have a straight 5f.

Grade: E (but form from the all-weather surface is not reliable on grass)

Effect of the draw: Except on the 5f straight course, low numbers are much the best. Anything drawn wide tends to lose ground on the bends.

Success rate of all favourites: 28.6 per cent.

Favourites' success in two-year-old stakes: 31.5 per cent.

Trainer tip: The runners of J. Pearce are worth noting; most of his winners are horses of four-years-old or more.

THIRSK

Left-handed. A flat, oval 1m 2f track, there are sharp turns and a 4f run-in. The straight course is 6f long.

Grade: C

Effect of the draw: High numbers are definitely favoured in sprint races, except in soft or heavy ground. Low numbers have the edge up to a mile on the turning course.

Success rate of all favourites: 31.2 per cent.

Favourites' success in two-year-old stakes: 30.6 per cent.

Most significant form: (1st, 2nd, 3rd, 4th last time out) from Thirsk itself.

Trainer tip: Sir M. Stoute, H. Cecil and J. Dunlop are the 'big three' for stakes and weight-for-age races. The superior class of runners from their yards nearly always tells, *whatever the indications in the betting market.*

WARWICK

Left-handed. A circular 1m 6f course with a 2½f run-in. The 5f track is dog-legged.

Grade: E

Effect of the draw: Low numbers do best on good or faster ground because the course's left-handed bends favour them. When the ground is really soft on the other hand, high numbers are favoured in all events up to a mile as the ground up the stands' rail is then much faster.

Success rate of all favourites: 31.3 per cent.

Favourites' success in two-year-old stakes: 46 per cent.

Trainer tip: B. Hills has a fine record, although his juveniles have not done very well in recent seasons.

WINDSOR

Right-handed. A very flat 1m 4f figure-of-eight track with sharp turns, it has a long run-in of 5f, giving the galloping types plenty of time to get balanced for the finish. The 5f 217yd track is not quite straight.

Grade: D

Effect of the draw: Sprinters drawn high are clearly best, but only if the ground is good or fast. Soft going favours low-drawn horses.

Success rate of all favourites: 28.6 per cent.

Favourites' success in two-year-old stakes: 33.3 per cent.

Most significant form: (1st, 2nd, 3rd, 4th last time out) from Windsor itself.

Trainer tip: Sir M. Stoute has a good record in handicaps from relatively few runners.

WOLVERHAMPTON (ALL-WEATHER)

Left-handed. This oval course is only 1m long and with a straight of about 2f, it obviously has very sharp bends. The fibresand surface is the slowest of all British all-weather surfaces. The 1m 2f turf track runs outside the fibresand, with a 4½f run-in and a straight 5f course. It is not used at present.

Grade: E (but form from the all-weather surface is not reliable on grass)

Effect of the draw: None on grass, but on the all-weather a horse which can come up the centre of the course seems to be at an advantage, unless the surface has been recently harrowed, when low numbers are favoured at the bends.

Success rate of all favourites: 29.3 per cent.

Favourites' success in two-year-old stakes: 34.1 per cent.

Trainer tip: W. Jarvis does exceptionally well in conditions races.

YARMOUTH

Left-handed. A 1m 5f oval circuit with a 5f run-in, the course is flat and favours big, long-striding horses. All races up to 1m are on the straight course.

Grade: C

Effect of the draw: High numbers have always been favoured on the straight track, but recent changes to the course may have destroyed or altered the bias.

Success rate of all favourites: 34.2 per cent.

Favourites' success in two-year-old stakes: 47.9 per cent.

Most significant form: Top two-year-olds from the big Newmarket yards often make their debut here.

Trainer tip: Runners in the Godolphin colours are not frequent but they currently have a 45 per cent strike rate.

YORK

Left-handed. This is a 2m horseshoe-shaped, galloping track with a 5f run-in. There is a straight 6f and a chute for races over 6f 214yd.

Grade: A

Effect of the draw: Low numbers are best in all races up to 6f 214yd, especially on soft or even heavily watered ground.

Success rate of all favourites: 27.9 per cent.

Favourites' success in two-year-old stakes: 36.4 per cent.

Most significant form: (1st, 2nd, 3rd, 4th last time out) from Newmarket. All the handicaps at York are exceptionally tricky because of the keenness of the competition there. The form from York, where the best horses from the north and the south meet, is very reliable. The May meeting in particular is one of the best guides to the near future in the racing calendar.

Trainer tip: No trainer stands out at this most competitive of venues, but J. Dunlop's two-year-olds have been outstanding in recent years and M. Johnston makes a speciality of winning nurseries.

National Hunt

As with the Flat, all course gradings are unofficial. National Hunt Flat form is included in the winning percentages for all favourites but, because of the problems associated with races of this type, they are excluded from the recommendations for best and worst races for favourites. The latter are not based solely on winning percentages or the level-stakes profit or loss position. In all cases a recommendation has been arrived at by taking into account both these factors in relation to one another against the background of other relevant form factors. Similarly, the trainer tips are not necessarily for handlers with the highest strike rates or best profit figures. Other factors bearing on both the past and the future have been considered in framing them.

AINTREE

Grand National Course: Left-handed. This is a flat circuit of 2m 2f with 16 extremely stiff fences, despite repeated modifications. There is a long run-in of 494yd with an elbow.

Mildmay Course: Left-handed. A sharp, flat course of 1m 4f, the fences are only of average difficulty. There is a run-in of 260yd. Front runners are favoured.

Grade: A

Success rate of all favourites: 36.3 per cent.

Best races for favourites: Hunter chases 64.3 per cent. Novice chases 58.3 per cent.

Worst races for favourites: Handicap hurdles 21.9 per cent.

Trainer tip: H. Johnson sometimes lands a coup in chases.

ASCOT

Right-handed. This triangular course of 1m 6f is level and enables horses to gallop freely but is still testing, with very stiff fences. The uphill finish of 160yd adds to the difficulties.

Grade: A

Success rate of all favourites: 32.6 per cent.

Best races for favourites: Weight-for-age chases 66.7 per cent. Hunter chases 45.5 per cent.

Worst races for favourites: Handicap hurdles 25.8 per cent.

Most significant form: (1st, 2nd, 3rd, 4th last time out) from Cheltenham and Newbury.

Trainer tip: G. B. Balding has, on average, better than 25 per cent of winners to runners over a number of recent seasons, with a sound level-stakes profit from all runners. He does best in chases, both novice and handicap, whilst his handicap hurdlers are also invariably well placed.

AYR

Left-handed. A 1m 4f fair, flat, galloping track. Fences slightly more severe than average, but there is no water jump. There is a run-in of 210yd.

Grade: C
      B (Scottish National meeting, April)

Success rate of all favourites: 36.2 per cent.

Best races for favourites: Hunter chases 62.5 per cent. Weight-for-age chases 50 per cent. Weight-for-age hurdles 45.5 per cent.

Worst races for favourites: Handicap chases 32.3 per cent.

Most significant form: Form from the Grand National meeting at Liverpool is untrustworthy at the big April meeting here.

Trainer tip: P. Nicholls has few runners but a very good percentage of winners and overall shows a level-stakes profit for the indiscriminate backer. His hurdlers, however, are especially successful.

BANGOR-ON-DEE

Left-handed. A 1m 4f round, turning course with sharp bends. All hurdle races are run on the inside track of the circuit. The fences are of average difficulty. The run-in is a long 325yd. The track favours handy types and front runners. The ground can become very testing making it foolhardy to support a horse whose fitness is in doubt.

Grade: E

Success rate of all favourites: 33.5 per cent.

Best races for favourites: Hunter chases 42.9 per cent. Novices chases 40.2 per cent.

Worst races for favourites: Handicap hurdles 24.2 per cent.

Trainer tip: The runners of N. Twiston-Davies should be noted.

CARLISLE

Right-handed. A 1m 5f stiff, undulating circuit with average-size fences. The uphill run-in measures 250yd. Stamina is essential on a course that does not drain well in periods of very wet weather.

Grade: D

Success rate of all favourites: 38.6 per cent.

Best races for favourites: Novice hurdles 46.5 per cent.

Worst races for favourites: Weight-for-age hurdles 28.6 per cent.

Most significant form: (1st, 2nd, 3rd, 4th last time out) from Carlisle itself.

Trainer tip: Mrs M. Reveley is the dominant trainer in all kinds of race.

CARTMEL

Left-handed. A sharp, undulating track of just over a mile with testing fences. The 800yd run-in is the longest in the country. Cartmel favours small, handy horses.

Grade: E

Success rate of all favourites: 35.9 per cent.

Best races for favourites: Novice chases 47.1 per cent.

Worst races for favourites: Handicap hurdles 22.4 per cent.

Trainer tip: P. Bowen leads the way with a strike rate of well over 40 per cent and a good level-stakes profit from his relatively small number of runners. Horses travelling north from M. Pipe's stable should also be noted – the West Country maestro wins roughly one race from every two attempts here.

CATTERICK

Left-handed. A sharp, oval track of 1m 1f which is wider and not quite so tight as the Flat course. The fences are easy. There is a run-in of 240yd. Well-balanced front runners perform well.

Grade: D

Success rate of all favourites: 36.8 per cent.

Best races for favourites: Handicap chases 46.3 per cent.

Worst races for favourites: Handicap hurdles 17.4 per cent.

Most significant form: (1st, 2nd, 3rd, 4th last time out) from Catterick itself.

Trainer tip: Most of the big northern trainers regularly score here but only J. J. O'Neill even begins to challenge Mrs M. Reveley's dominance at her local National Hunt track.

CHELTENHAM

Left-handed. This is a 1m 4f oval track with extremely stiff fences. There is a testing, uphill run-in of just over 350yd on the Old Course. The New Course finish is half a furlong less at 237yd, again up the famous hill. Horses must stay every yard of the trip to score.

Grade: A (Old and New Courses)

Success rate of all favourites: 34.9 per cent.

Best races for favourites: Weight-for-age hurdles 49.1 per cent. Hunter chases 44.4 per cent.

Worst races for favourites: Handicap chases 25.8 per cent.

Most significant form: (1st, 2nd, 3rd, 4th last time out) from Newbury. The first half-dozen home in the Thomas Pink Gold Cup in November are usually worth following for the rest of the season.

Trainer tip: No trainer can really be said to have the edge in any type of race at jumping's most competitive venue but Miss H. Knight's runners are invariably well placed and start at value prices.

CHEPSTOW

Left-handed. A 2m undulating, oval course with a very long straight. Fences are of above-average difficulty. The downhill run-in is 240yd long. The going is often very testing.

Grade: B

Success rate of all favourites: 34.1 per cent.

Best races for favourites: Novice chases 44.3 per cent. Weight-for-age hurdles 43.2 per cent.

Worst races for favourites: Handicap hurdles 23.2 per cent.

Most significant form: (1st, 2nd, 3rd, 4th last time out) from Cheltenham.

Trainer tip: The top trainer at the track, in percentage terms, is P. Hobbs. His hurdlers are preferred to his chasers as betting propositions.

DONCASTER

Left-handed. The flat, galloping track with easy bends inside the Flat course is 2m long. The fences are of moderate difficulty and there is a run-in of 250yd.

Grade: B

Success rate of all favourites: 34.5 per cent.

Best races for favourites: Novice hurdles 61 per cent.

Worst races for favourites: Handicap chases 29.8 per cent.

Most significant form: (1st, 2nd, 3rd, 4th last time out) from Newcastle.

Trainer tip: North meets south on this very easy course. M. W. Easterby is the best of the home side, but winners from the south come from a wide range of yards.

EXETER

Right-handed. This is a hilly 2m course. The fences are slightly above average and the run-in is of 250yd.

Grade: D

Success rate of all favourites: 34.7 per cent.

Best races for favourites: Novice chases 40.2 per cent.

Worst races for favourites: Handicap chases 32.1 per cent.

Trainer tip: The Pipe/McCoy combination reigns supreme. Well-backed, but relatively unexposed horses are their speciality here.

FAKENHAM

Left-handed. This almost square track of about 1m is sharp but the fences are easy. There is an uphill run-in of 220yd.

Grade: E

Success rate of all favourites: 38.8 per cent.

Best races for favourites: Novice chases 43.1 per cent.

Worst races for favourites: Handicap hurdles 34.1 per cent.

Trainer tip: O. Brennan is nearly always highly competitive with his steeplechasers at this Norfolk venue.

FOLKESTONE

Right-handed. This is an easy track of 1m 3f with easy fences and no complications. The run-in is about a furlong for chases, slightly more for hurdles.

Grade: D

Success rate of all favourites: 41.7 per cent.

Best races for favourites: Novice chases 55.6 per cent. Novice hurdles 48.4 per cent.

Worst races for favourites: Handicap hurdles 24.6 per cent.

Trainer tip: Hurdle race candidates from the yard of Mrs M. Jones have chalked up a number of successes from not too many runners. Miss V. Williams and N. Henderson are two top trainers with a high strike rate in all kinds of race.

FONTWELL

Left-handed. The hurdle course is a tight oval of 1m round. The chase course is a figure-of-eight. The fences are moderate and the run-in is 230yd. The horses-for-courses theory works here.

Grade: D

Success rate of all favourites: 40.4 per cent.

Best races for favourites: Handicap chases 45.8 per cent.

Worst races for favourites: Handicap hurdles 25.3 per cent.

Trainer tip: Hurdlers from the stable of Miss V. Williams can be trusted to run well at reasonable odds.

HAYDOCK PARK

Left-handed. It is a 1m 5f flat, oval course with the hurdles track inside the chase course which, in turn, is inside the Flat circuit. The drop fences are very severe. There is a long run-in of 440yd. A fair but tough test.

Grade: A

Success rate of all favourites: 44.3 per cent.

Best races for favourites: Novice hurdles 53.6 per cent. Handicap chases 45 per cent.

Worst races for favourites: Novice chases 33.3 per cent.

Most significant form: (1st, 2nd, 3rd, 4th last time out) from Newcastle and Wetherby.

Trainer tip: On a course which has always been good for fancied horses, N. Richards often lands a coup, whilst Miss V. Williams and Mrs S. Smith are two lady trainers with exceptionally consistent records.

HEREFORD

Right-handed. A 1m 4f square course. The fences are moderate. A 300yd run-in from the final fence is slightly downhill. It is an easy circuit where speed is at a premium.

Grade: E

Success rate of all favourites: 36.8 per cent.

Best races for favourites: Novice hurdles 42.9 per cent.

Worst races for favourites: Weight-for-age chases 12.5 per cent.

Most significant form: (1st, 2nd, 3rd, 4th last time out) from Worcester.

Trainer tip: Watch out for Miss V. Williams's chasers and her better-class novice hurdlers.

HEXHAM

Left-handed. A 1m 4f undulating course. The fences are of average difficulty. The home straight is on the climb with a run-in of 250yd, making this a testing track.

Grade: E

Success rate of all favourites: 33.9 per cent.

Best races for favourites: Novice hurdles 46.8 per cent.

Worst races for favourites: Handicap chases 24.4 per cent.

Trainer tip: The stable of J. Quinn is usually on the mark with its hurdlers.

HUNTINGDON

Right-handed. A flat, oval 1m 4f course. Some of the fences are of above-average difficulty, and there is a run-in of 200yd. The long-striding animal who can race up with the pace is admirably suited here.

Grade: C

Success rate of all favourites: 40.7 per cent.

Best races for favourites: Novice hurdles 45.9 per cent. Novice chases 44.4 per cent.

Worst races for favourites: Weight-for-age chases 25 per cent.

Trainer tip: M. Pitman could well go on to consolidate his gains in races of all kinds.

KELSO

Left-handed. This is a tight, oval track with part of the hurdle course inside the main circuit of 1m 3f. The fences are of above average difficulty. Sharp turns disadvantage the galloping types. There is a long, stiff, uphill finish of 490yd from the final fence.

Grade: E

Success rate of all favourites: 40.6 per cent.

Best races for favourites: Hunter chases 51.9 per cent. Novice chases 48.6 per cent.

Worst races for favourites: Handicap chases 29.4 per cent.

Trainer tip: Mrs A. Swinbank's hurdlers have an excellent record and may continue to show an overall profit.

Kempton

Right-handed. A flat, triangular circuit of 1m 5f. The fences are stiff. Short run-in of 200yd accentuates the fact that speedy types are much favoured.

Grade: A

Success rate of all favourites: 38.8 per cent.

Best races for favourites: Novice hurdles 38.4 per cent.

Worst races for favourites: Handicap hurdles 21.4 per cent.

Trainer tip: N. Henderson averages one winner a meeting once the stable hits form.

Leicester

Right-handed. This very undulating, sharp, oval course is 1m 6f long. The fences are quite demanding. There is a run-in of 250yd. This is a searching test and because the going can get very heavy in winter it adds to the rigours imposed by the course.

Grade: D

Success rate of all favourites: 37.3 per cent.

Best races for favourites: Weight-for-age hurdles 57.1 per cent.

Worst races for favourites: Handicap chases 21.5 per cent.

Trainer tip: West Country travellers from the M. Pipe yard are statistically head and shoulders above the rest. K. Bailey likes to bring on useful young horses here.

LINGFIELD PARK

Left-handed. A round track outside the Flat circuits measuring 1m 7f. The fences are slightly above-average difficulty. A 200yd run-in. The course is one for well-balanced horses and course specialists.

Grade: B

Success rate of all favourites: 42.9 per cent.

Best races for favourites: Weight-for-age hurdles 58.9 per cent.

Worst races for favourites: Handicap hurdles 22.2 per cent.

Trainer tip: The ubiquitous M. Pipe is likely to remain the trainer to follow.

LUDLOW

Right-handed. A 1m 4f oval course. The fences are of moderate difficulty and there is a long run-in of 450yd. This flat track has sharp bends at the entrance and exit to the straight.

Grade: E

Success rate of all favourites: 36.5 per cent.

Best races for favourites: Hunter chases 46.4 per cent. Novice hurdles 43.1 per cent.

Worst races for favourites: Handicap hurdles 28.2 per cent.

Trainer tip: N. Henderson's winners are plentiful and profitable here. Strangely for a yard noted for its hurdlers, the chasers have the better overall record.

MARKET RASEN

Right-handed. A 1m 2f oval course which is sharp and undulating. The fences are moderate in difficulty. The run-in is a furlong in length. Handy sorts are best, with horses up with the pace likely to score if good enough.

Grade: D

Success rate of all favourites: 33.4 per cent.

Best races for favourites: Weight-for-age chases 80 per cent.

Worst races for favourites: Handicap hurdles 21.6 per cent.

Most significant form: (1st, 2nd, 3rd, 4th last time out) from Market Rasen itself. The form works out badly at this 'farmers' meeting' where many of the lesser lights of the jumping game do not get too much competition from the top yards.

Trainer tip: Miss H. Knight's infrequent visits to the track must be noted. Her runners have a sound record in most types of races, giving an overall strike rate of 34.1 per cent.

MUSSELBURGH (EDINBURGH)

Right-handed. A sharp 1m 2f oval course with quite hard fences. The run-in is only 150yd long. Adaptable horses are obviously favoured.

Grade: E

Success rate of all favourites: 34.1 per cent.

Best races for favourites: No specific recommendation.

Worst races for favourites: Novice chases 21.3 per cent.

Trainer tip: L. Lungo leads a small number of northern trainers who dominate proceedings at this seaside track.

NEWBURY

Left-handed. A level, galloping track. It is 1m 7f in length, lying inside the Flat circuit. The fences are severe and there is a run-in of 255yd. It makes for a fair test of a jumper but horses lacking in courage are soon found out.

Grade: A

Success rate of all favourites: 37.3 per cent.

Best races for favourites: Hunter chases 57.1 per cent. Weight-for-age chases 46.2 per cent.

Worst races for favourites: Handicap hurdles 25 per cent.

Most significant form: (1st, 2nd, 3rd, 4th last time out) from Ascot.

Trainer tip: M. Pipe's runners do well in every type of race and, at this important venue, prices are well above average for the stable.

NEWCASTLE

Left-handed. This is a 1m 6f oval, galloping circuit with testing fences and a run-in of 220yd. The home straight is uphill.

Grade: B

Success rate of all favourites: 41.2 per cent.

Best races for favourites: Novice chases 52.7 per cent.

Worst races for favourites: Handicap chases 31.8 per cent.

Most significant form: (1st, 2nd, 3rd, 4th last time out) from Ayr.

Trainer tip: Training honours are shared out fairly equally here at Gosforth Park, but Peter Niven is the 'job' jockey favoured by many of the shrewdest betting stables in the north.

NEWTON ABBOT

Left-handed. Another flat, oval course, it is only 1m 1f with tight bends. The fences are of moderate difficulty. The run-in is 300yd and the track is ideal for the quick, well-balanced runner.

Grade: C

Success rate of all favourites: 38.9 per cent.

Best races for favourites: Weight-for-age chases 67.3 per cent. Novice chases 46.8 per cent.

Worst races for favourites: Handicap chases 33.5 per cent. Hunter chases 33.3 per cent.

Most significant form: (1st, 2nd, 3rd, 4th last time out) from Newton Abbot itself.

Trainer tip: K. Bailey's runners are equally good here under both codes, hurdling or steeplechasing.

PERTH

Right-handed. The flat circuit is just over 1m 2f in length. The fences are fairly easy. The run-in is 300yd in hurdle races and 450yd on the chase course. The bends are very tight and badly inconvenience the galloping type of animal.

Grade: E

Success rate of all favourites: 36 per cent.

Best races for favourites: Novice chases 45.8 per cent. Hunter chases 45.5 per cent.

Worst races for favourites: Weight-for-age chases 25 per cent.

Trainer tip: Raiders sent north from P. Hobbs' yard shine in all kinds of race.

PLUMPTON

Left-handed. A small, tight course of 1m 1f with sharp bends. The fences are fairly easy. The back straight is all downhill, but a stiff, uphill finish 200yd from the last bend makes this a difficult course to negotiate. It thus favours track specialists.

Grade: E

Success rate of all favourites: 36.7 per cent.

Best races for favourites: Novice hurdles 47 per cent. Novice chases 43 per cent.

Worst races for favourites: Handicap chases 27.4 per cent.

Most significant form: (1st, 2nd, 3rd, 4th last time out) from Plumpton itself.

Trainer tip: N. Henderson does not send all that many horses to the Sussex course, but both his hurdlers and his handicap chasers should be looked at very closely.

SANDOWN PARK

Right-handed. An oval course, it is about 1m 5f in length. The fences are quite severe and there is a testing uphill run-in of 300yd which favours front runners which see the trip out.

Grade: A

Success rate of all favourites: 46.5 per cent.

Best races for favourites: Hunter chases 66.6 per cent. Novice hurdles 57 per cent.

Worst races for favourites: Handicap hurdles 17.2 per cent.

Most significant form: (1st, 2nd, 3rd, 4th last time out) from Ascot.

Trainer tip: The hurdlers of P. Hobbs have an outstanding recent record at this high-class track.

SEDGEFIELD

Left-handed. This is a sharp, oval track of 1m 2f with average fences. A 3f downhill run to the final obstacle is followed by a tough 200yd climb to the finishing post. It is another course where horses with winning form at the venue continue to do well.

Grade: E

Success rate of all favourites: 35.6 per cent.

Best races for favourites: Novice chases 47.3 per cent. Hunter chases 46.7 per cent.

Worst races for favourites: Handicap hurdles 26.1 per cent. Weight-for-age hurdles 27.3 per cent.

Trainer tip: Trainers from Co. Durham and Northumberland have a superb record at their local track. F. Murphy's fencers are worth noting.

SOUTHWELL

Left-handed. The turf course inside the all-weather track is only 1m 1f in circumference. Fences are average. The run-in is 250yd long and the course is extremely tight, especially for chasers.

Grade: E

Success rate of all favourites: 33 per cent.

Best races for favourites: Novice hurdles 51.8 per cent.

Worst races for favourites: Handicap hurdles 20.8 per cent.

Trainer tip: W. Turner makes a speciality of winning hurdle races at this East Midlands venue. His strike rate is currently 55.6 per cent and the profit to a level stake is well in excess of 50 per cent.

STRATFORD

Left-handed. This is a sharp, flat, triangular course of just over 1m 2f where the fences are moderate. The run-in is 200yd long.

Grade: C

Success rate of all favourites: 33.6 per cent.

Best races for favourites: Weight-for-age hurdles 45.5 per cent. Hunter chases 44.7 per cent.

Worst races for favourites: Weight-for-age chases 25 per cent. Handicap hurdles 25 per cent.

Trainer tip: Miss H. Knight's hurdlers average one win from three runs.

TAUNTON

Right-handed. A flat, oval track of 1m 2f, cambered to offset the tightness of the bends, with an uphill run-in of 150yd. The ground tends to be very heavy in winter but can become extremely firm at either end of the National Hunt season.

Grade: E

Success rate of all favourites: 41 per cent.

Best races for favourites: Novice hurdles 66.3 per cent.

Worst races for favourites: Handicap hurdles 14.9 per cent.

Trainer tip: Local handler K. Bishop's few runners are suggested as an alternative to the M. Pipe winner machine. Among the latter's many winners here, however, there are usually some at reasonable prices.

TOWCESTER

Right-handed. This 1m 6f undulating, square circuit is set out on the side of a hill. The first half is downhill before a long climb over the final 6f leads to a run-in of 200yd. Though the fences are no more than moderate, this is a severe test of a jumper.

Grade: D

Success rate of all favourites: 33 per cent.

Best races for favourites: Hunter chases 51.4 per cent. Weight-for-age-hurdles 41.9 per cent.

Worst races for favourites: Handicap chases 26.4 per cent.

Trainer tip: Miss V. Williams has the knack of winning with her chasers. Prices on the whole represent reasonable value.

UTTOXETER

Left-handed. This is an easy, galloping oval of 1m 2f with average fences. The level run-in is only 170yd long. Front runners do well in hurdle races.

Grade: D

Success rate of all favourites: 35.2 per cent.

Best races for favourites: Novice hurdles 45 per cent.

Worst races for favourites: Weight-for-age hurdles 12.5 per cent.

Trainer tip: L. Lungo has a high rate of success from a small number of runners.

WARWICK

Left-handed. A circular course of just over 1m 5f, with quite sharp bends. The fences are on the stiff side. The run-in is 240yd long.

Grade: C

Success rate of all favourites: 35.8 per cent.

Best races for favourites: Weight-for-age hurdles 48 per cent.

Worst races for favourites: Handicap chases 23.2 per cent.

Trainer tip: M. Pipe leads in every department with his chasers currently winning more than one race in two. Miss V. Williams is the other trainer to follow in steeplechases.

WETHERBY

Left-handed. A 1m 4f elongated track, there is a long, steady rise to the finish. The fences are severe. The run-in is fairly short at 190yd. The hurdles course, which is inside the chase circuit, is quite sharp. A stiff but fair test of a jumper, the course attracts a very good class of animal.

Grade: B

Success rate of all favourites: 43.5 per cent.

Best races for favourites: No specific recommendation.

Worst races for favourites: Handicap chases 38.7 per cent.

Trainer tip: C. Grant is currently the man to follow over both sorts of obstacle. His runners are not all that plentiful but his success rate with them is very high.

WINCANTON

Right-handed. A 1m 3f galloping track, its fences are quite testing. The run-in is 200yd long.

Grade: B

Success rate of all favourites: 34.4 per cent.

Best races for favourites: Novice chases 44.1 per cent. Weight-for-age hurdles 42.2 per cent.

Worst races for favourites: Handicap chases 24.7 per cent.

Trainer tip: P. Nicholls heads affairs in all departments with a high percentage of winners and a level-stakes profit overall.

WOLVERHAMPTON

Left-handed. This pear-shaped track is outside the all-weather circuit. The fences are moderate and there is a run-in of only 180yd.

Grade: D

Success rate of all favourites: 51.5 per cent.

Best races for favourites: Novice hurdles 55.6 per cent.

Worst races for favourites: Handicap hurdles 33.3 per cent.

Trainer tip: There is very little National Hunt racing at the Midlands venue these days, but the course is still on M. Pipe's hit list. His hurdlers especially run well and even indiscriminate betting on them has produced a profit in recent seasons.

WORCESTER

Left-handed. This is a flat, galloping track of 1m 5f. The fences are moderate and the run-in is a furlong in length.

Grade: C

Success rate of all favourites: 35.3 per cent.

Best races for favourites: Novice hurdles 42 per cent. Novice chases 40.8 per cent.

Worst races for favourites: Handicap hurdles 29.6 per cent.

Trainer tip: K. Bailey has an excellent record with all kinds of horse.

Index